Jacob Bronowski: Selected Poems

Simon Rennie
Editor

Jacob Bronowski: Selected Poems

palgrave
macmillan

Editor
Simon Rennie
Department of English and Creative Writing
University of Exeter
Exeter, UK

ISBN 978-3-032-19596-8   ISBN 978-3-032-19597-5   (eBook)
https://doi.org/10.1007/978-3-032-19597-5

Foreword

Jacob Bronowski: The Soul in Singleness

Those, like me, who come from the generation that encountered Bronowski on the small screen through his pioneering BBC documentary *The Ascent of Man*—still believed by many to be the greatest series of films of its kind ever made—will welcome this opportunity to discover his poetry. He wrote verse throughout his life and the adventure before us here is to follow the voice of Bronowski as the terrible twentieth century unwinds from the late 1920s through to the 1970s.

I had the good fortune to get to know Alistair Cooke a little, the writer and broadcaster best known for his long-running series of *Letter from America* for the BBC. He told me a story about his first day at Jesus College, Cambridge, where, a nervous scholarship boy, he had arrived in 1927. He sat in his panelled rooms unsure what to do or where to go when a knock came at the door. A young student with remarkable eyebrows bobbed in and introduced himself.

> "My name's Bronowski. You play chess?"
> "Er, yes. Yes, yes I do."
> "Oh good. Come up to my rooms."

A chessboard was already laid out. Cooke sat down and Bronowski said, "Oh. Before we begin. What sort of game do you play? Classical or romantic?"

Cooke told me that at this question his worst fears about Cambridge were instantly realised. He was doomed, he saw, to be dwarfed and humiliated by the kind of towering intellectuals who talk casually about classical and romantic chess styles…

In fact of course he and Bronowski became fast friends[1] and Cooke found to his relief that other undergraduates were far from as forbiddingly gifted. Cooke

---

[1] Also, 40 years or so later—how could they have guessed it?— Cooke's *America* was to form the second panel of the triptych of pioneering, world-class documentary film series that began with

was there to read English Literature, Bronowski to pursue a degree in Mathematics (he was to get the university's highest first-class degree in the subject, conferring on him the title 'Senior Wrangler'). Cooke went on to edit the university's *Granta* magazine. Bronowski ran, along with William Empson, *Experiment*, a literary periodical. *Literary*, note, not mathematical. Empson was reading mathematics too. He would go on to become a highly regarded poet and perhaps the foremost literary critic of his age, but like Bronowski he started out as what Cambridge calls a 'Mathmo'.

For a very long time the division between the arts and sciences has been a running sore for academics and intellectuals. In the 1950s and 1960s Cambridge was to see a famous and rather acrimonious 'Two Cultures' debate between C. P. Snow and F. R. Leavis as well as the production of books like T. R. Henn's *The Apple and the Spectroscope* and Aldous Huxley's essays in *Literature and Science* which all tried in different ways to anatomise the relationship, close to enmity at times, and bridge the gap between what appear to be two fundamentally different ways of looking at, investigating and interpreting the world. Whether Empson encouraged Bronowski in the belief that poetry, mathematics and the material sciences were all one, or whether it was Bronowski who encouraged Empson, I cannot tell. Perhaps they each were born fully armed with minds that found it easy to straddle and enrich both fields.

The scientific and the poetic soul can imagine themselves united in William Blake's famous stanza:

> *To see a world in a grain of sand.*
> *And a heaven in a wild flower.*
> *Hold infinity in the palm of your hand.*
> *And eternity in an hour.*

Bronowski all his life was a passionate lover and ardent defender of Blake and those lines surely do speak as clearly to a scientist as to an artist, for this way of perceiving and interpreting—of reading truth from the evidence of the actual and the particular—is as much a poetical as a scientific practice.

Blake's grand image of Isaac Newton leaning down to draw geometrical shapes with a compass is brought to mind in Bronowski's self description in his poem 'Revenge'. It makes very clear his trinitarian sense of coexistent, consubstantial identity as poet, man and mathematician.

> *Man and geometer, I*
> *read truth to be a finesse*
> *made greater than nobility, and, poet,*
> *that the adherence to truth is*
> *no faculty, but is the soul*
> *in singleness, and in being whole.*

Kenneth Clark's *Civilisation* and was followed by Bronowski's *Ascent of Man*. All the brainchild of BBC 2's Controller, David Attenborough.

poet, man, geometer, I am headstrong in this.

What a wonderful last phrase! Simultaneously self-confident and self-mocking.

The idea we have to dismiss straight away is the sentimental and wholly inaccurate one that might imagine Bronowski using poetry to 'express himself' and to release a looser, less forensic and materialist side to his personality. Far from it: I think we find clearly in the poems here that he sees the poetic process as congruent with the scientific and mathematical. What is a thing? What is its nature, its essence, its truth? If the thing is a rock, a gas or a cell then—yes, instruments such as a microscope might be used and the power of numbers deployed, but if it is an emotion, a historical event, a sight in nature, then the instrument is a pen and the power of words is deployed. But the project remains the same—to find the truth inside.

The poems here tend to be loosely but not rigorously formal in their metre, using predominately 'slanted' or half rhymes. At first—if we read this collection in chronological order—we encounter poetry that is clever, complex, jerky and compressed. Jerky? Is that an insult or a compliment, I wonder. Well, as in much of the poetry of his friend Empson, the sense is that of a poet feeling for apprehension and answers, fighting to put ideas and images together in a truthful way. So there are many run-ons and breaks in the lines—enjambments and caesuras as they're known in the trade. Hesitations abound and clauses are nested into each other. Lyrical poetry it is not. He does not contrive sustained and complex metaphors in the manner of John Donne, George Herbert, Andrew Marvell or the other 'metaphysical' poets. Nor is he as naive in his language and image making as his beloved William Blake. But while you can detect elements of both Donne and Blake in the poems (and later W. H. Auden too), from the very beginning it is clear that Bronowski has his own very individual voice, his idiolect. We quickly notice he has his store of favourite words too: 'medlar', 'brunt' (particularly as a verb), 'dung' and 'boor'.

For me the collection really comes to life as the 1930s (Auden's 'low dishonest decade') builds into war and worse. By Chap. 3 the allusions and references grow to the Spanish Civil War (he had a particular affinity for and love of Spain) to Guernica and especially to the deaths of four great artist intellectuals he greatly admired, Karl Kraus, Garcia Lorca, Ernst Toller and Erich Mühsam. The last three perished at the hands of Fascism, Toller by suicide and Mühsam by torture, while Lorca was shot and killed by Franco's militia. Kraus was saved from a similar inevitable fate by a heart attack in 1936.

Perhaps my favourite of Bronowski's poems is 'The Great', a bitter denunciation of the failure of his contemporaries to live up to the greatness of past poets and artists. France, England, Ireland, Italy, Germany were once 'lit' by the greatness of Degas, Dryden, Yeats, Dante, Goethe and more. "But all that ends. The lands which blazed, burn out." The relevance to our own times, as authoritarianism rises all around Europe, Asia and the Americas, of this poem and others, is aching and acute. But he finds optimism too:

> *The fable ends in hope, the leaf*
> *Shall live, the locusts shall retreat.*

There is great pleasure and satisfaction to be derived from spending time in such civilised, intelligent, wise and passionate company. The breadth and depth of Bronowski's mind is always apparent, but the shuttling between doubt, despair and hope, the probity with which emotions and postures are examined, and the sincerity of his gaze all reveal a humble, modest, human and authentically poetic soul. I am headstrong in this.

© Stephen Fry 2025

London, UK   Stephen Fry

Acknowledgements

I am deeply indebted to Jacob Bronowski's surviving family, but especially Judith Bronowski and Clare Bronowski, for encouraging this project and providing vital context and information in fascinating conversations. Equally fascinating and helpful conversations were had with John Hare and Professor Nicholas Jardine which helped shape the direction of this book from an early stage.

Respective archivists at Jesus College, Cambridge, Robert Athol and Rob Payne, were equally considerate in enabling me to carry out research into the Bronowski holdings.

CONTENTS

CHAPTER 1

Introduction

Jacob Bronowski (1908–1974) is widely regarded as one of the last great polymaths, having been prominent in the fields of philosophy, mathematics, science, and literary criticism. To many people he is known as the creator of the successful 1973 BBC television series, *The Ascent of Man*, and the bestselling book that accompanied the programme. However, alongside his scientific and broadcasting pursuits, Bronowski wrote and occasionally published poetry throughout his adult life. While studying mathematics at Cambridge in the late 1920s and early 1930s his literary associations included William Empson, John Davenport, T. H. White, Kathleen Raine, the future broadcaster Alistair Cooke, and the future film actor Michael Redgrave. In the years before the Second World War Bronowski was deeply immersed in European poetic culture, forming literary friendships with figures including Samuel Beckett and Robert Graves. From files held in the archives at Jesus College, Cambridge it is clear that in the early 1940s Bronowski had gone some way to assembling his own work into a collected edition. This volume represents a posthumous revival of this project, while also including later post-war poems, some of which featured in home-produced Christmas cards sent out to a wide circle friends and acquaintances. There are more Bronowski poems than the 107 collected here. This selection is intended to be fulsomely representative rather than actually exhaustive.

A Brief Biography

Among other sources I am chiefly indebted for this section to Timothy Sandefur's 2019 biography *The Ascent of Jacob Bronowski: The Life and Ideas of a Popular Science Icon* (Prometheus Books). Summarising Bronowski's life into just a few paragraphs is a difficult task. To declare that Jacob Bronowski was

S. Rennie (ed.), *Jacob Bronowski: Selected Poems*,
https://doi.org/10.1007/978-3-032-19597-5_1

more than just a poet is not to diminish the body of work, but it is nevertheless something of an understatement. Few people in the twentieth century could claim to have had so much impact on so many various fields of endeavour. Yakob Bronowski was born into a Polish Jewish family in Łódź in 1908 (although it may have been late 1907 by some accounts), when that city was technically situated in the Polish Congress, part of the Russian Empire. His father, Abram, oversaw part of the family textile business, which had manufacturing bases in Łódź and London, where the family would eventually settle. However, due to various factors including economic pressures and political instability (which included antisemitic attacks on the Jewish population in Polish regions), the Bronowski's moved to Plauen in Saxony in 1911. It was here that Yakob received his first official education, in German, at the Höhere Bürgerschule. After the end of the Great War, political instability again caused the family to move in 1920, this time to London's East End. At twelve-years-old, Yacob spoke no English (he retained a distinctive European accent throughout his life), but this was not unusual for new arrivals in this vibrant working-class Jewish area of Britain's capital, and the family soon integrated itself into the local culture. Yacob, eventually Anglicised to 'Jacob', attended the Central Foundation Boys' School, where he excelled in academic studies. In 1926 his prowess in mathematics led to him being awarded a Cambridge scholarship, and the following year he began to attend Jesus College.

It is at Cambridge that the particular blend of scientific and humanities pursuits that would be forever associated with Jacob Bronowski began to develop. Alongside excelling in his geometrical and algebraic studies and earning a half-blue for his brilliance at chess, Bronowski, familiarly known since his school-days as 'Bruno', embedded himself into the literary culture of the university. Alongside the future broadcaster Alistair Cooke, he sat for a while on the editorial board of the literary magazine, *Granta*. In 1928 he co-founded and co-edited a more specialised modernism-focussed literary magazine, *Experiment*, whose first edition (it ran for seven) included his own poems and literary criticism alongside the works of William Empson, John Davenport, T. H. White, Michael Redgrave, Hugh Sykes, Arthur Tillotson, and Kathleen Raine. He also began to publish work in other magazines involved in the development of British literary modernism during the period including the *Cambridge Review* and *This Quarter*. In 1929 the publishers W. Heffer & Sons published six pamphlets edited by Bronowski and James Reeves (who was also part of the team that produced *Experiment*) containing individual poems under the series title *Songs for Sixpence*. The contributors to the *Songs for Sixpence* series of pamphlets were William Empson, Julian Bell, T. H. White, John Davenport, Michael Redgrave, and Bronowski himself. In the summer of 1930 Bronowski travelled to Paris, where he met James Joyce (whose poetry subsequently appeared in an edition of *Experiment*) and Samuel Beckett. Bronowski and Beckett maintained a friendship for a while and Bronowski included his and Joyce's work in his edited volume of an anthology called *European Caravan* in 1931. Bronowski graduated as 'Senior Wrangler' (best mathematician) in

1930, and completed a Cambridge doctorate in mathematics in 1933, during a period when he and his then girlfriend, Eirlys Roberts, were occasionally staying at the house of Robert Graves in Majorca. The couple had befriended Graves (1895–1985) and his partner, the American poet and critic Laura Riding (1901–1991) in the summer of 1932. Roberts, a classical scholar, helped Graves with the historical details of the manuscript of his novel *I, Claudius*, while Bronowski and Riding worked on an ambitious, and ultimately doomed, scholarly dictionary project. Relationships eventually became strained, and Graves would subsequently write a vindictive poem satirising Bronowski's social and intellectual ambition. It was originally entitled 'A Portrait of Little Jacob' (Bronowski was famously diminutive in stature) but later published in the 'Satires and Grotesques' section of his collection *Poems 1938–1945* (Farrar, Strauss and Giroux, 1946) as 'Dream of a Climber'. The poem contained the line 'nosings of pure brass', which can be interpreted as an antisemitic reference, despite Laura Riding's status as a Jewish writer and her and Graves's early identification of T. S. Eliot's antisemitism in their work *A Survey of Modernist Poetry* (1927).

Despite his stellar academic achievements, Bronowski failed to attain a teaching post at Cambridge, and in 1934 he acquired a position teaching mathematics at the University of Hull, an institution later to provide employment for another poet, Philip Larkin. He held his position at Hull until 1942, publishing poetry in the university poetry magazine, *The Torch*, and a group of poems on the subject of the Spanish Civil War ('Guadalajara', 'The Death of Garcia Lorca', 'Greece and Spain', and 'Bomber') in the pamphlet *Spain 1939: Four Poems*, produced by the Hull-based Andrew Marvell Press in 1939. The *Spain 1939* and *Songs for Sixpence* pamphlets represent Bronowski's only dedicated original poetry publications, but 1939 also saw the Cambridge University Press publication of his first full book, a critical monograph entitled *The Poet's Defence*. This work, an answer to the isolating formalist New Criticism of I. A. Richards (1893–1979) and others, was an attempt to 'write criticism as reasoned as geometry' (*The Poet's Defence*, p.8) and sought to define poetry using the critical writing of poets including Philip Sidney, Percy Bysshe Shelley, John Dryden, William Wordsworth, Samuel Taylor Coleridge, Algernon Swinburne, A. E Housman, and W. B. Yeats. The thesis of this volume was provocative, but the historical sweep of its source material was characteristic of Bronowski's ambition, and of his tendency to universalise. Late in 1938 Bronowski had met the Jewish artist and sculptor, Rita Coblentz (who published some of her work under the surname 'Colin'). After his relationship with Eirlys Roberts ended, Rita and Jacob developed a bond which would last for the rest of his life, and they married in 1941.

While working at Hull Bronowski attracted the attention of the British secret services, and a file was created on him as a possible subversive, or worse. It is also not difficult to see that, in the paranoid political pre-war environment, Bronowski might have appeared a likely candidate for communist recruitment. He was Eastern European, Cambridge-educated, vocal in his support for the

Spanish Republicans, and his intellectual mother, Serla (eventually Celia) Bronowski, actually was a member of the Communist Party. It would also not be untypical if elements of antisemitism were not a factor in the British establishment's perspective on an overachieving Jewish intellectual. In reality, Bronowski's politics were always more moderately leftist, with his political involvement largely limited to his literary associations. Despite pre-war suspicions, he was eventually recruited in 1943 on the basis of his unique mathematical abilities to join the Allied 'RE8' organisation of strategic operations, which used scientific principles to predict the effects of blanket bombing, developing military offensive and civilian defensive responses. Alongside celebrated mathematicians including John von Neumann, Bronowski's research informed recommendations for the effective Allied aerial bombardment of mainland Europe. It was this role, and that as part of the post-war British scientific team that travelled to Japan to report on the effects of the atomic bombs dropped on Hiroshima and Nagasaki, that helped to inform Bronowski's later philosophies on the relationship between science, morality, and the imagination. Alongside his work for the military, 1944 saw the publication of his second monograph, *The Man Without a Mask*, another work of literary criticism, this time focussed on William Blake, and the birth of his and Rita's first child, Lisa Anne. The Blake volume, published by Secker and Warburg, was a critical success; it was praised by W. H. Auden and V. S. Pritchett, and became a significant text in Romanticism studies.

This success in the field of literary criticism for a man still in his mid-thirties might have led to a career based on professorial appointment, but Bronowski's post-war story is characterised by his refusal to be pigeon-holed. His career pathways' influence on the development of his ideas on scientific humanism makes sense retrospectively, but from the mid-1940s his intellectual eclecticism only intensified. In 1945 he was Scientific Deputy to the British Chiefs of Staff Mission to Japan and produced a seminal report, *The Effects of the Atomic Bombs at Hiroshima and Nagasaki*. He was still engaged in post-war government research when he was loaned to UNESCO to lead its Project Division in 1947, having a significant effect on the future direction of the newly created global organisation. The year before, in 1946, Bronowski had first been invited to appear on the panel of the popular BBC radio programme, *The Brains Trust*. The show already featured such philosophical luminaries as Bertrand Russell and Julian Huxley, but Bronowski's abilities as a broadcaster led to him eventually becoming the programme's lead philosopher, as panels discussed moral and philosophical issues in response to audience questions. Bronowski consolidated his radio broadcasting profile by also being one of the first contributors to the hugely influential BBC national radio station *The Third Programme*, which remained at the centre of British artistic cultural discussion throughout its broadcast history from 1946. In 1950 Bronowski was recruited as director of the Central Research Establishment of the National Coal Board, where he would work for over a decade and invent the famous (but commercially unviable) 'Bronowski's Briquettes', also leading the team that developed smokeless fuel. He managed hundreds of researchers, but the role still allowed time for his other pursuits. It was also in 1950 that Bronowski saw his most successful radio play, *The Face of Violence*, broadcast to great acclaim on BBC radio. The work explores the quest for revenge of a former prisoner of war, framed as a realist study with divine philosophical commentary. The play won the Prix Italia in 1951, and in that year his first non-literary book was published, *The Common Sense of Science*. Not only did the public perception of Bronowski's talents broaden further, but he began to hone what would eventually be his most identifiable attribute, as an unrivalled public interpreter of complex scientific and philosophical ideas. In the early 1950s Bronowski was asked to use his geometric and statistical talents to help establish whether the famous Tuang Child skull (discovered in South Africa in 1924) should be classified as simian or hominid. Although his report became caught up in the occasionally vicious scientific debate around the classification of the fossil, it would eventually contribute to the artefact's acceptance as an example of the early hominid *Australopithecus*. More than this, the experience of working on early human history would provide an important platform for the intellectual questions later addressed in *The Ascent of Man*.

Through the 1950s Bronowski's reputation in US intellectual circles grew, fuelled partly by the philosophical impact of works such as *The Common Sense of Science* and 1956's *The Science of Human Values*, and his association with American institutions began to develop. In 1953 he held the Carnegie visiting professorship at MIT in Cambridge, Massachusetts, but from 1960 he was involved in the foundation of the Salk Institute for Biological Studies with Jonas Salk (1914–1995), who had developed the first Polio vaccine, and the molecular biologist who had co-discovered the helical structure of DNA, Sir Francis Crick (1916–2004). Bronowski's administrative experience at the National Coal Board stood him in good stead during this period, and he was instrumental in the architectural design of the Salk Institute's campus in La Jolla, near San Diego. The Bronowski family, minus daughters Lisa and Judith who remained in England to attend university, moved to a house in La Jolla in 1964. The Bronowskis' three surviving daughters, Judith, Clare and Nicole, still live in the US. The Institute's status as part thinktank, part research institute, eminently suited Bronowski's catholic approach to intellectual pursuits and he remained an associate director until the end of his life. Many of the notes towards poems created in the last decade of his life are scribbled on Salk Institute headed note paper. However, at the beginning of the 1970s Bronowski was granted 3 years leave from his duties at the Institute in order to research and film his mammoth BBC TV series, *The Ascent of Man*. He was already familiar to British television audiences from documentaries on William Blake and Leonardo da Vinci, but *The Ascent of Man* was a hugely ambitious undertaking, intellectually and televisually. In some ways, it served as a companion piece to recent BBC programmes *Civilisation: A Personal View* (1969) made by the historian Kenneth Clark, and *America: A Personal History of the United States* (1972) made by Bronowski's old Cambridge associate, Alistair Cooke.

The main thematic difference was that while the former concentrated on art, and the latter on history, Bronowski's series incorporated the history of science, and examined human culture and achievement through its understanding of science. The programme was first broadcast in the UK in May 1973, and its impact was instantaneous. Its scope allowed for Bronowski's many fields of interest to coalesce into the expression of a unified philosophy, its generous (for the BBC, at least) budget enabled filming in global locations, and perhaps most distinctively, Bronowski improvised many of the monologues which held the programme together. This latter element gave the series a balanced sense of scale, intellectual curiosity, and intimacy which was, and arguably still is, unmatched. Even today, more than half a century on, many consider the programme the apotheosis of popular science broadcasting. The accompanying bestselling book, the majority of whose prose is taken verbatim from the programme's scripts, has been through several editions. The series was first shown in the US in 1975, but sadly Jacob Bronowski was not able to enjoy its transatlantic reception. He died of a heart attack on the 22nd of August 1974 in New York, having suffered from coronary issues for a few years. He was 66 years old.

This Volume

The main substance of this book consists of Bronowski's own arrangement and revision of his work dating from 1928–1940, with additional texts drawn from later periods including the Christmas card poems, which continued almost annually for the remainder of his life from 1939. When gathering his poetry Bronowski undertook major rewrites of his previous work, some of which had been published in newspapers or literary magazines, and as discussed below, these revisions are incorporated into this volume. Most poems are provided with an exact date of composition because Bronowski kept an appointments diary (held at Jesus College) which noted his social and literary practice, including the writing of poems. The largely pre-war work was arranged into three sections by Bronowski, chronologically covering poems written or published in 1928–1931, 1931–1936, and 1937–1940, and these make up Chaps. 2, 3 and 4 in this book. Most of the poetry from Chaps. 3 and 4 was earmarked by Bronowski in the early 1940s for a standalone collection which never appeared entitled *Thumb in The Margin*. Poetry was produced more sparsely in the period after this, but there are twenty-nine Christmas card poems which Bronowski composed from 1939 to 1973, which are presented in Chap. 5. These cards, famous among the couple's wide circle of friends and acquaintances, showcased Bronowski's poetry alongside his wife Rita's artwork. There is also a selection of miscellaneous poems dating from 1939 through to the end of Bronowski's life, which makes up Chap. 6. The volume concludes with an explanatory appendix offering notes on the provenance and publication contexts of each of the poems, along with information about the extent of revision undertaken by the author where it is relevant. For some works the poem's topic or form is briefly discussed, but this is intended to be descriptive rather than analytical. Because the publication profiles of the Christmas card poems are consistent, these pieces are discussed as a group in the appendix.

Although I am a literary scholar with a particular interest in poetry, my motivation for editing this volume has been more personal. When I first met my partner, Rachel Jardine, in 2019, we discussed our heritages and the fact that we were both Jewish through our mothers' lines. When Rachel revealed that her mother's maiden name was 'Bronowski' I naturally asked, 'like Jacob Bronowski?', to which Rachel replied 'well, *actually* Jacob Bronowski – he was my grandfather.' Like many people of my generation, Jacob Bronowski (always known as 'Bruno' to family and friends) was to me a humanist hero, a figure uniquely placed between science and the humanities. His eclectic achievements in philosophy, anthropology, and literature studies had inspired some of my interests. My own limitations meant I found his mathematical work largely incomprehensible, but a hardback copy of *The Ascent of Man* had been sitting on my bookshelf for as long as I could remember. Bruno died before Rachel was born, and sadly, his eldest daughter, the well-known historian Lisa Jardine (1944–2015), died before I met Rachel. Nevertheless, I met Bruno's surviving daughters, Judith, Clare and Nicole, online during the Covid pandemic, and on subsequent trips out to California where their father had moved with the family in 1964 to work at the Salk Institute. As a literature academic I was familiar with Bronowski's work on William Blake and his contribution to the Philip Sidney/Percy Bysshe Shelley critical legacy with his monograph *The Poet's Defence* (1939). However, although potted biographies would sometimes describe him as 'mathematician and *poet*' I could find very little evidence of his poetry beyond snippets of quotations and second-hand biographical references pertaining to his undergraduate days at Cambridge in the late 1920s and early 1930s. Conversations with Rachel and the family revealed that, though a significant body of work existed, it had never been collected. Perhaps Bronowski's wide-ranging but startlingly successful subsequent career pathways diverted him from his literary endeavours, but it seemed extraordinary that this unique modernist voice had never really been heard. This anomaly only became more apparent when I collected and read the poetry and fully appreciated its fascinating conversations with humanism, literature, and politics. These conversations reflect their historical moments, but also speak to today's concerns, sometimes in quite stark terms.

Bronowski's papers are held in the archives at his *alma mater*, Jesus College, Cambridge, and along with letters and other documents, the poetry is only a relatively small part of it. Although they are organised very well, the poems are presented in a variety of forms, typed and handwritten, sometimes on plain or lined paper, sometimes as hand-edited cuttings from publications. The author undertook extensive revision of most of his work, attesting to his serious consideration of eventual publication. There are no true examples of juvenilia in the holdings. Or rather, much of the earliest poetry there was written when he was an undergraduate, and it had been published in volumes including the college magazine, *Experiment, Songs for Sixpence,* the *Cambridge Review*, and *New Writing*. Later publications included the Hogarth Press volume *Poems for Spain* (1939), and in magazines such as *Granta* and *Ambit*, but even so, most of the poems presented in this volume are previously unpublished. And indeed, given that Bronowski subsequently revised almost all of his previously published verse, few of these poems have been read in the form in which the author eventually intended. Very little poetry appears to have been written during the Second World War, and the gaps between the poems written after the war are noticeably longer. It is significant that several of the poems in Chap. 6 of this volume are untitled, indicating if not an unfinished status, then a less probable readiness for publication. For these pieces I have assigned titles in square brackets based arbitrarily on first lines, as per convention.

Editing

While fair copies of some of Bronowski's poetry in the Jesus College archives exist, many of the texts remain in a less publishable form. Bronowski's own revision of his previously published poems also presented something of an editorial challenge. I took the decision early in the process of editing that I should be as true to the author's apparent wishes as possible. Therefore, I endeavoured to incorporate as accurately as possible the handwritten revisions into the versions featured in this volume. While this would be standard practice for the publication of manuscripts of unpublished poetry, it is more unusual to work in this way for poetry which has made appearances in previous publications. But in this case, few of the published poems were widely read, with most of the early work appearing in well-respected but culturally esoteric magazines with small print runs. Many of these have yet to be digitised, meaning that public, or even scholarly, access to the majority of Bronowski's poetic output is extremely limited. In addition, it was clear from the extent to which Bronowski reworked copies of previously published poetry that he was at some point intending to present his work as a coherent whole. While Bronowski's handwritten revisions made transcription, and in some cases interpretation, difficult, it also allowed for a rewardingly deep immersion into his poetic method through the editorial process. His editorial tendency was to cut rather than to add, but unlike other examples of poetic auto-revision such as the retrospective meddling of Bronowski's contemporary W. H. Auden (1907–1973) or the Victorian Chartist Ernest Charles Jones (1819–1869), these changes rarely affected the poems' ideology or meaning. Rather, these are examples of a mature poet improving the work of his younger self, tidying up the rhythm, and subsequently achieving a more direct and distinctive poetic voice. The extent to which poems are revised differs widely, with some barely changed and others extensively rephrased. Several times, poem titles appear to have been changed retrospectively, and I have indicated where this occurs in the appendix. However, in almost all cases the motivation behind these revisions appears to be aesthetic rather than semantic or political. A different editorial challenge presented itself in relation to the later, post-war poetry. There was less revision in evidence in this mostly previously unpublished work, and some of the hand-written poetry appeared to lie somewhere between the status of note form and fair copy. I took the decision to only select work where there was enough care in the author's handwriting to suggest a personally acceptable version.

One area where Bronowski's authorial practice assists the editor is in his record-keeping. As noted above, almost all the poetry copies, whether in typed or handwritten form, are accompanied by notes detailing the date of composition. Often this is the exact date, but sometimes just the month. This is especially useful when reading occasional poetry alongside its historical context or for establishing the order of poetic sequences. Because in most cases on the typescripts the notes detailing the dates appear to be handwritten after the fact, I was at first a little sceptical of, or at least curious about, the accuracy of these claims. It was only when examining Bronowski's assiduously kept appointment diaries in the Jesus College, Cambridge archives that all became clear. Most completed compositions are noted in these diaries, providing a creative record which is unusually historically specific. Bronowski also often provides hand-written information in relation to publication, but this is sometimes apparent anyway from the context. Indeed, many of the early poetry copies consist of pages torn from the original publication (in *Experiment* or *Songs for Sixpence*, for example) with handwritten revisions made directly onto the page. The handwriting style is distinctive but legible in most cases, with fairly consistent and standard annotation figures indicating line shifts or stanza break changes. The author was clearly making notes towards intended future publication.

THEMES

As one would expect for a selection of poetry written across six decades, the subject matter of Bronowski's poetry varies, ranging from the lyrical and intro-spective to explicitly political works that document current affairs through a poetic imaginary. A few of the works are more or less explicitly autobiographi-cal (with the long piece 'Thumb in the Margin' being very much a case of the former), while others adopt an ostensibly impersonal voice. There are sympa-thetic elegies on figures such as Y. B. Yeats (1865–1939) and Frederico Garcia Lorca (1898–1936), but there is also a coruscating unpublished condemnation written shortly after the death of Pope Pius XI (1857–1939), a figure Bronowski clearly viewed as effectively appeasing European fascism. While Bronowski's poetic voice is remarkably consistent in its register across his oeuvre, there are discernible phases. The early works from the university publications *Experiment* or *Songs for Sixpence* are quite abstract, clearly in conversation with contempo-rary modernist writers including T. S. Eliot and H. D., as well as his fellow Cambridge students William Empson, John Davenport, and Hugh Sykes Davies. From the early 1930s, with the advent of the Spanish Civil War and the broader rise of European fascism, political works feature more, and indeed this political engagement never entirely leaves Bronowski's poetic approach—his very last poem (probably) comments on the 1970s Watergate scandal. His late 1930s poetic preoccupation with the Spanish Civil War (obviously coloured by his sojourns at Robert Graves's Majorca home at the beginning of the decade), and the rise of fascism in general, might be seen to mirror Auden's similar observations, but Bronowski is less didactic than his modernist contemporary. His work also seems more focussed on the cultural appeal of right-wing populism and nationalist ideology than Auden, and poems including 'The Word', 'The Gangster', 'Take Your Gun', and 'The Impersonal Tragedy' can be read as eerily relevant to a range of political issues in the third decade of the twenty-first century.

Bronowski also did not exclude economic political critiques from his poetry. Composed just before the outbreak of the Second World War, the unpublished 'War and Peace', despite its playful riddle-like form, is a sardonic reflection on the fact that whatever the geopolitical situation, it is the worker who pays the bill. It begins with the lines 'Peace, he smokes a big cigar;/picks your pocket— or was it war?', which features the cigar as a left-wing symbol of capitalist complacency. But the later lines 'Peace is blander, war kills faster:/two names, but a single master' suggest a cynicism that sees war, at least in economic terms, as merely an acceleration of prevailing political intent. Composed just 2 weeks before this, and apparently looking already beyond the coming conflict, 'Our Age is Beginning' is a more optimistic but also more specifically class-conscious piece, offering a celebration of the achievements of the working class in forging the future. Here 'the common man has fingers so fine/that all the world is his design', and the future relies not on the artist or the policy maker, but on 'the driver in his cabin' and 'the precision of mechanics'. While this valorisation of 'ordinary' people perhaps comes as no surprise from a left-leaning intellectual in the 1930s, its apparent vision of the postwar cultural landscape reads almost presciently in relation to the eventual cultural, if not political, prominence of the British working classes in the 1950s and 1960s.

Although Bronowski only refers specifically to his Jewishness in two of the poems collected here ('The Death of W. B. Yeats' and 'Thumb in the Margin'), and his consistent variety of interests meant he was not engaged in any sustained way with Jewish literary culture, many of his poems can be read productively through the lens of his ethnic identity. Peter Lawson, in his 2006 study *Anglo-Jewish Poetry from Isaac Rosenberg to Elaine Feinstein* notes that 'Anglo-Jewish poetry tends to follow a Romantic tradition. This is a universalistic tradition of affiliation with the outsider, the dispossessed and others passed over in silence' (p. 1–2). Quite apart from the rather obvious observation that Bronowski's poetry has been effectively silenced by neglect for many decades, even while his other cultural achievements have been celebrated, it is tempting to see Bronowski's affinity with William Blake in light of this 'universalistic tradition'. Blake was an outsider in his own lifetime and also in his literary legacy until his work was championed by Dante Gabriel Rossetti and Swinburne many years after his death. But he also, like Bronowski, was not just a poet, and saw his work as part of a much broader schematic concept. This might have been spiritual-political, while Bronowski's was philosophical-scientific, but both men sought to universalise their creative practices.

Lawson also encourages recognition of the tendency for Anglo-Jewish poetry to engage with radical, rather than conservative approaches, referring to descriptions by the Anglo-Jewish poet Jon Silkin (1930–1997) of 'romantic' language which 'sensuously enacts', as opposed to 'formal' language which 'narrates' (p. 12). It is possible that had this volume been available when Lawson was developing his study, Bronowski might have been included alongside Rosenberg, Siegfried Sassoon, John Rodker, Silkin, Karen Gershon and Elaine Feinstein. He would certainly have warranted an honourable mention. Like Gershon, Bronowski was born in mainland Europe but came to Britain as a child, but the poet among these he perhaps most resembles is John Rodker (1894–1955), who Lawson describes as a 'minority modernist'. Like Bronowski, Rodker is known for something other than his poetry—he was responsible for publishing editions of T. S. Eliot's *Ara Vos Prec* (1919), Ezra Pound's *Hugh Selwyn Mauberley* (1920), and Joyce's *Ulysses* (1922). But Rodker also shares Bronowski's secular approach and his occasionally visceral language. Lawson quotes an obviously antisemitic letter from Wyndham Lewis to Pound describing Rodker as a 'poisonous little bugger', which reminds us of the casual antisemitism of modernist figures including Lewis, Pound, and indeed Eliot (p. 77). With Graves's 'Dream of a Climber' poem as the most explicit example, this serves to contextualise Bronowski's place in the British modernist pre-war environment. Incidentally, it is Lewis whom Bronowski identifies as bringing Hitler to the attention of British readers in 1931 in his explanatory note for the poem 'Crisis' (see appendix). While some critics have read Rodker's work more through the lens of English modernism, Lawson suggests that '[w]ithout my emphasis (on his Anglo-Jewish status), many resonances from Rodker's poetry would be lost' (p. 193). This might usefully be applied to Bronowski's poetry. On a purely linguistic level, it is worth bearing in mind that, like masters of Anglophone literature Joseph Conrad (1857–1924) and Vladimir Nabokov (1899–1977), English was not Jacob Bronowski's first language.

Even if Bronowski were not *Bronowski*, with all his many achievements culminating in the cultural behemoth *The Ascent of Man*, the unread poetry of this Jewish Polish immigrant to Britain warning of the rise of European fascism, demagoguery, and right-wing populism in the 1930s would deserve a modern audience. The fact that most of this poetry has barely been read combines with the multiplicity of his achievements, experience, and one might even say *identities* to present the reader with a complex of historical and biographical contexts with which to engage. However, notwithstanding Bronowski's critical opposition to formalist approaches to poetry, perhaps the first task of the reader is to simply read the poems as they are, and this book's first function is to enable this.

Simon Rennie, Axbridge, Somerset, Autumn 2025.

CHAPTER 2

1928–1931 (Collected Poems)

Seascape

I
When evening is a blue marsh,

and the sea
is mist, dulling the west
with silver;

when the flight of gulls
hangs on the twilight
quivering arches,

as the gulls wheel
with a cry
bellies fired suddenly
by the sunset;

when the tide swells

and swings out to the moon
softly, through the west

burning:

in the evening
I have strained for beauty.

S. Rennie (ed.), *Jacob Bronowski: Selected Poems*,
https://doi.org/10.1007/978-3-032-19597-5_2

II
Not loveliness,
as the grace of gulls trembling
in spirals;

dusk, or the high tide faltering,
like a drift of petals
through windless gardens:

but beauty that comes riding
suddenly, with a shouting of breakers.

III
Not the twilight
whose shadows flower darkly,
parched for thunder -

but when night
touches the cliff,

knotting in dark sinews
the strain of stone to stone,

for a vision of apocalyptic beasts
scarred there;

when the oxen of the maned cliff
tread out the night mightily,
with folded wings

their hoofs trampling
the shallows,
and the starlight
pointed in the seadeep black:

then beauty rises,
tense
as the drums
of some dark pulse
in the night.

BETRAYAL: A BIOGRAPHY

1 <u>Spring is the end</u>

It lacquers the coffin with sunlight
a painted strut to the lid,
or finer steel the candles' quivering.
There birds' beaks shrill the song
on the ribbed house,

where once old men beside the wall
fell silent, when visions
mumbled their end to them.

Did they see Taranis's
ship in thunder drawn home
with its wheel restless?
The swans were going down
to the western cry of water sunset-lapped,
in the moan
and silver sobbing of the prow,
when the wave turned and faltered again and failed.

Did they see Taranis trapped
with slaves at the mill
turning the steel spokes,
wheel over wheel
crying, whose scattered rust
muttered the end,

thunder, or at the last
only a coughing
which shakes the dark?

But the young men
pucker sympathetic eyes
and ties blue-flowered,
their conversation
echoes earth tumbled back
when wheels on the gravel go home
perhaps motor-ships
discharging filmy dazzle --

"Isn't this oil gorgeous at sunset
And the rising moon."

This oil is nitreous, barred with iron's
corruption. Its Castle-soap
trickles with a heavy sound.

2 <u>Question of Autumn</u>

Perhaps it was the dead --
their leaf
(elm, oak, mahogany
or mistletoe)
spun in slow oaths
to silence,

Hödr that forged death
or Loki the dry twig's fire --

first said treason.

Or the wind that whispered
a tired steeling spring,
the swans homing
to the shuttered house.

Was it autumn that withered the flesh,
only ribs survived of the leaf
and jagged trees as disused drainpipes,

(slow sap the sun
drained on the northern water)

or fate on the window
when the branch taps
death, the mistletoe?

The treason was not theirs
nor was it Balder was betrayed
though his youth was broken. But Hödr
trapped, and blind at the forge,
his metal twisted to strange corruption,
him they betrayed.

3 <u>Mediterranean Honeymoon</u>

In the sun's sluices
steams the sea-anneal,
that hisses at pierheads'
banked white flame

like fever
or a vaguer mist of musk.

The vision is Roncesvalles
when the dark fires come from Saraguce
with the cry of scythes
and the horn moans again
and whispers, and dies --
long ago?

Who knows?
Only one voice now divides
fire from flame;
making excellent
mystery of marriage;

though it speaks through cigarette-haze
yet wakes it
the leaping burn
of the Caucasus,
it sweeps about
Marsilie, Marsilie,
like a horn:

"Leaving the gravel
when the moon's slow

loveliness made paler
the green April,"

and its silence
was faun-laughter.

Over the woodwind sea
can you not hear that horn
on steel struts' moon-bewitched echoes
die, the cry
Roncesvalles?

4 <u>Midsummer Dance</u>

Between the shaven armpits,
the patent leather, and music,
over, over,
the horn essays its slower storm-wings,

"The Scythians swore by wind and sword."

In corn and negro-minstrel mouthing
hear, Adonis falters,
Ares, sworded, for a moment cordless
in woodwind triumphs.

"When did the nightingale,
when did the nightingale
in Caroline
and Chinese springs, wheels and counterpoise,
leave the old king
lonely for gramophones,
when did the nightingale die?"

So a moment we lilt the treason
which feeds the wind
and moonlight-bright jazz --

and Adonis rises,
Aphrodite is lavish, Artemis –

Ares is chained again at the gate.

It is over, as slowly and again
we aspire the horn-hollow streets,

Adonis, Adonis!
And Ares is an impotent Scythian.

5 <u>Winter Moon</u>

Now underfoot, which is crisp snow,
the moonlight cages him by rail and railing
who remembers her face first on its side
wax-flat, and terrible
in pain like stone:
remembers her face that watched
limply the dusk, that whispered.

I was bound, was it then,
or in the singing half-leisurely when
Helgi, Helgi sought her,
Diana, or as cold a woman?

"Who is pale, she is pale,
when sea most murmurously trails
the veil dusk, the soft sails.
on failing water,
she is pale."

In that sea
what current drew silver
on her lidless eyes,
and purple of oil barred

with Hödr's metal, gold of Taranis,
the chains that Ares strained;
its wind too trapped,
slowly from the horn Roland bleeds.

And at the last Helgi,
he too broken with the unstable moon,
in silver chains is hobbled,
there the still, the swaying
grove or sea-grot
cried for blood
when the branch shook;
Dag struck.

Now stilly, stilly
it is the end to the bonds
which strangled godhead;
so we shall fail.

Stilly until shall steel of Odin's dagger
bleed a soft rust
about her shoulders, sea-dragged;
until staring Diana shall,
turning, be sudden white;
and the woodwind plaint, exigent, follow the horn.

SERENADE

Shall I make songs
about you;
telling the heart to be still:

shall I say

"Her loveliness
is a veil
twisted
to strangle love"

"Yesterday
she was dawn,
she was noon,
and now
she is more splendid than the evening"

or

"Her flame rages about me,
I am white ashes
and how shall the heart survive?"

Shall I make songs
about you,

saying

"I loved her
once";

or be still,
breaking the truth
with no word.

HER LIPS

I said
"Not dream-beset
her lips
are trees that stir in the darkness,
her kisses whisper
and fail."

I said,
"There are no dreams
burning there;
to-morrow I shall be parched with other lusts."

It is evening again;
passionless the lamplight caresses my lids
where your kisses
were morning rain;

and the shadows
tighten over my throat,
your mouth was a whip there
and your lips -

what was the scent of them,
tangled in elder and birch once,
what were their dreams -

your lips are masts
bearing the memory outward.

CITY SUMMER

I could hear silence now,
like snow, falling,
that the ear echoes
and forgets.

If silence pricked this restless
drone, suddenly,
a star in the heat – darkness -

silence under the ice
and in the long arches of snowdrifts -

breaking
the exigence, to and fro
sweltered, and street-mouthed echo,

I could hear it
tighten
like a tree to the rime,
or a bird's wing
that splinters the frost.

OCTOBER CASUISTRY

We come to the fall of the year:
kingdoms tremble.
The triumph drawing through the town
is cohorted with a new multitude,
with the leaf's rusting,
its chariots
lay the past summer dust, apt, aquarially.

Now princes fold away their youth
their bronze congeals, municipal, statuesque,
rust is their sleep

of which, who shall say whether they'll stir again
before the swallow dares?
All this winter when no leaf,
only the slowly shaken bough,
stirs the deep pools of the wind
we shall remember that wheel
which the sun's
tight focus of faith once spun -
ground now to nebulae, or casual haloes.
The princes
standing in the squares shall be afraid at night.

They are patient, though all their certainty was gone, that those
would be an end, with steady fetlocks treading.
Like them, follow
this penance triumph -
as dry, as brittle crackling brass,
and as unfamiliar,
though snow-deep in the winter street.

To Juliet, in the Tomb

I
Now's your resurrection,

for winter slips from the land,
the graves uncover.
They were tulips but the new year
breaks, breaks and bares them,
lipless; the throats of daffodils in spring.

From buds shut against late snow grows autumn,
from that again the daffodils,
though winter locked their sleepless grieving
into the bulb.
So long these, that are changeable, bleach and age:
May and the twelvemonth to June,
till spring returns slenderly
rustling among the months, for they are
his incorruption they're beginning
and end, ear unto seed, when from the harvest,

a fifth season.

II
Now's your resurrection,

Yet you dreamed of spring
and trembled.
Juliet, who so uneasy with the dead
that in the darkness
a daydream shakes you?

Was then death so kind, to
to give your lids a little
sleep, to draw fibres or roots,
your hair as thin shoots among boughs not yet green?

Life had been many times
moving your hands for others,
from balconies, its promise evening to overtake you
with the bearing of sons for a quarrel
of noblemen. Also passion -
whose end was at graves: you heard stir near,
its whisper catacombed the dark.

Thus death was beautiful because it came once
and shook torch-crimson over you and took you from others
for a night. -
How many shoulders bruised your burying?
That's not to question.
Solitude and the
privacy of
parks answer it: you are content
to have slept in royal tombs.

III
Now's your resurrection,

though your be sleep difficultly undone
as tulips or
spring,
not they, not the magnificence of
lids greedy of death
shall flinch the folding back.
You have lived,
Juliet, splendid among the dead.
Now learn, rising, the forgotten gait
of spring to summer,
unlamped streets and silent
solicitation. Was winter so good, that plumy burial?
Lift your rich lashes

and strip your lips of death,
no blood upon your mouth now -
suck back the honey of your breath, queen,
the time for dying is past:
you, Juliet, who fell back dead
once.

PRAYER

Tighten, Astarte, my lids,
that I have, who died
a year ago, burial.
And I will make flutes of my bones, flags my
flesh, in thanksgiving.
Let me put off these womanly garments
and uncover again the scar
with which once I ran through the streets and shouted.
Goddess, think back to that time
when the now broken vessels were my vigour;
before I sat propped against a gate
with the sun over my shoulder, or the night,
and where my mouth was, wind.
Locusts brought their dry thighs
to cover me, heat to eat my hands,
their trickle speared bone heat
to pound my blind hollows.
Yet Astarte, goddess, think of the night when I lay still by you,
though I knew there would be this morning;
when I looked up and saw the scarlet
drawn over my eyes, my throat which you had
drained out and broken between your hands;
I was not afraid.
You chose me, made me barren,
and put me apart from those sleeping:
Be kind to my pride among them
and let me not be eaten up with them and the white ants,
or my flesh, once yours, be tattered by jackals.
But beat out my eyes and break my mouth at last,
which speaks out of you;
bruise me to dust, for you are my death,
and my lids gape for burial.

ODYSSEUS AS GOD OF LOVE

Those who came by siege, by forced marches,
by surrender and loot; stubbornly prevailed with you -
Odysseus sacker of cities, they have consented
your death in the dead time
when darkly is remembered all your burning.

Though it is hardly a memory, but hearsay
of trouble, uncertain, contrived –
now suddenly
upon the citadel of her eyes they mount,

upon her hands' towers,
her shoulders' fallen stone
whose gesture of turrets
was once sheer for your eyes' abandon;
where her heart burned are broken plains.

Because you were proud,
you marshal of an army with billhooks,
Odysseus a runner, a pricker of discontent
with paid pikes;

because cunning
upon the ramparts of her eyes -
for her spaces shouldered you,
her cone of sun was the spike
screwed to your shoes -

therefore, sweeping down like that remembered
darkly burning, you shall fall. Odysseus. You are only a bravo
fallen out of favour
by a covered bridge or a lane
and broken on the cobbles.
The tent's wing will cry for a moment after you,
after the trumpets. But the city still stands
in the last end, unsurrendered -
in the shrug of the watch
and while the dogs fawn on you, at your death.

FOR WILHEMINA

You have done well by water

Mandrake and anemone are your seasons
princess, the scarlet wound is breaking
tapers of pain, that the wind takes
and the sharp rain.

i
Iris betrayed us, fugitive, the month
budded and amazed, pointed in the throat
strangely. The pursed month
and broken and forgotten after rain.

We remember only thunder.
These were dark shaken over
waterflags, these were tulips
furled in the beginning mayed intrigued
discovered silver and the slant
treble upon crocus buds during March.

ii
You came among islands.
The wind stood in your sails
and the night but iris
grudging a coast.
We remember your coming
foretold with signs, stars, reason, with denial
(planned in a season of comets) abstinence.
The raw flesh, frayed at the nail,
shuddered on sea-lichens,

and much was granted; much was lost;
we remember
nothing withheld, certainly,
only the hands fumbling in flower throats,

your slight hands fumbling
abandon, and cherished pain, princess
of stemmed burnt starflowers
set in the slope of knees
outward, for desire.

Were these once certain,
was the mouth secret?
What shall be denied you,

foetus and fallen iris are your tokens
and lipless, perhaps lilies;
broken these mouths that labour
with a wind in spirals, bear dust;
and menstrual throats aching for rain.

iii
Now know that rain,
princess, over the islands,
and you coming among island
for star dust; for the fingered lust which
answers desire; among the unreal, illuminate pain
which is the air's, which gapes in the thigh.
We see your hands slightly
staunching where the womb leaps: unfruitful.
Which is their season?
And the answer wanders
bewildered the iris;
which asks for mandrake,
hollow only hears it echo, the anemone - your season.

PHYSIC

Physic will go behind the eyes,
there pit my thoughts:
for to the physic grey-glass drill
mining under my brow,
what's love but a soft peat?
But no physic will etch
your beauty out of my eyes.

No physic, which pricks
a place for aimless pain
that, growing local, it grow homely there.
For how shall physic shaft
what lies steady in my eyes
yet in them's nothing, nothing,
but your beauty? how mine that
which is no earth, nothing to strike?

FIFTH ARMY

Custom should be a house with the eaves deep,
and with stones easy again. This is my end,
the elms husband it.
There rain should fall of a Thursday,

and I should expect and forget it,
yet it would be given.

What lost this for me
when my father
and mother died with
the Hapsburgs?
My brother died in Leysin,
quickly after all, by a gash under the ear
in an iron pissoir.
He shouted the revolution

and had that comfort.
But who am I?
My sister. My sudden other self, also died,

stillborn, the incestuous blood
cried under my thighs
in a trench in Quentin in the dead watch.
Sweet uncleanness
why do I think of you,
stain at the eyes
of blood always?
I think of you in the gunsmells.
Why should the mind lie with the things past waking:
Courage, skill, gone a long time.
Sleep, the motions
that pieced a life.
But its remnants
fell to powder at Rheims.
When desire was pricked from the flesh like shrapnel,
yet swung out of the wet trench
and lived under the hand, roundly,
it wore pleasure like a hoop:

My sister, my sister
Whose body was smooth under the eyes
had no breasts,

now dances
in a speakeasy,
or in Janeiro in a gaminghell. Den of vice
dug under with trenches. Alien familiar
deaths bore her, my kindred.
In the end she had a sort of life;
bone three bloods - but changeable,

mulatto; dago with a dash of rumdrinking lowlands;
striped nigger that cherishes a little southblood.

The beating of guns
goes on as at the scab.
Custom, that's whisky
in barracks, a spilt quarrel,
or gin, that's adultery;
well now pernod
sneaks a little breath from pimping.

RETURN FROM DEATHS

1
Speak to me
when I am restless; who made
a grace of the occasion Tenderness,

one or two minutes
terribly, gave. Then break
the division of your lips,

and the eyes' visible round, so shored,
shrink: the thrust of islands
sharp, make upstart; stone against white Baltic.

2
I was born in the thaw-sullenness
with the mind of that air, bitter,
to mainland out: but the body
of the sea, unfriendly,

that under me in a stranger.
I inhabit you but my blood
is in Balchik in the butt of a street in Cluj
picked by snipers.

3
Was this to have been my life? with the falling
in Rumania: that I remember it

unthrift, shifting, in a grudging.
Out of changeable desire I was to have been the begetting,
from growth, stranger, into purpose

conceived for a stone's or pin inward into the
crunch and cast of the world; in the eddy flung down

as if against
the iris; rock-island,
of the inturned air, to prick upon the sea.

4
Well it was too hard. Forgive it me
which fear in the hand, that then grew a swimming-web,

loneliness, and the denying my birth,
make remember by night,

though I know they, who shared it,
would have died elsewhere,

at Czernowitz, the Black Sea,
in those ditches have been plundered beyond Sutmare,
lost stragglers in the marshes.

FRAGMENTS: FROM A POEM

Two turned; whispering, upon crutches
in a twisted stair -

       who saw:
What the eye takes. The mind rejects.
The word - the sense
answers - discards.
To one is known. Two cannot agree:

other two below them: gesturing.

Of the rainbrighted streets given back
grotesquely, these mutes changed
held in (holding) the leafed
beaten sustaining of lampgold thin thin
in a spindling fall of light out of metal
and the tension-fined film: flowering
sweet irreality, the two depths
(folded into one another) rounded
returning -

       little waters inexhaust;
and surfwhite of rainbeat
then white under gold;
the lake beats. This double hour
is begun.

That was clarity; perhaps this of the figures,
perhaps that; and arisen barely in speech: not speaking,
though when we saw her we had the illusion.
Hers is a kind of music

(under other spheres
spinning) the mind abandons it, haphazard,
nor was it needs fruitful, but
the late rain over the lake, purposeless,
changing in the light; gusty.
So the first word fell nowhere

                              sweet -
and the river slips.

Death was that in sweet water.
Then again music playing. Was mine
plucked from the fever of a June air her tune
a sinew; countertune; all beauty
for her, shrilly upon glass, and fluted
silver berries, the night's black juices.
Music, play. Play, Assyrian
Jewish or Ethiop maiden, tender
out of exile and loss, the sea's meshed strength
for lakesong, beaten
the bright scales of your body, Judea
in music, Philistia beat choking
when Dagon is out of the sea come again come
to spill his corporate eddy of nets
tightly over rivers.
Play, fighter with a trident
(steadily over the execution).

Why love do you
lean sadly to this? You are judged
by your pleasures, be glad we are lost tonight,
(and the homewaters remember them not)
when the floods come strangely
the nights are desired: fugitive among islands -

among reeds rain speaking,
always lakewater, there was no shore that night,
the lake sank into the stars, the islands
sank. We were lost.

TOURIST SEASON IN PARIS

This city is alive: that's strange that its device
lived in this weather,
when its crest fell. For the rain
runnelled and flaked it, made a summer down,
unbuoyant, which fell down. It had been splendid,
a heron trembling over
a kingfisher, brightness struck from the
declining water,
and a westering bird's
bellywhite in the flood-moon, waned Araris.
It lived in the air but then water
ran in the light; the silence
in which the blood had been aimless, trembling,
by no wing or wind shaken, gushed down. Like a hawk down
struck speech against the stranger speech; like land.
And made this city unwholesome, its isles gone to fester;
by night its gentle, most still voice
which, when voice is as light, was
shadow of light, made to a leprous scaly sound.
Malmaison is heard all day all that earth's speech; how is this city

(that was a heron flying over)
in its neckfeathers scragged away, bewildered
as a flight of quails is trivial augury.
They come like mothbirds,
heart, sound Heart, to your burning, orange, auspicious hill.

They see you alive, though whelmed once
by a deathly light out of Russia;
now comes over the Mississippi
their spring with green
birch-brightness, or virgin south's blue plague,
the silver leprosy. The gauds of the earth
come, gay spittled and rimmed bloody: for whom

Are not the rivers of Alaska? So gathered
the wheeling wheeling vulture omen
upon the quick of the air hangs, but in no fall of birds,
or beaky death over the gates the bird-clouds
on this dunged, grown fruitful city, are dropping
acrid richness. They are come over oceans
hawked on wrists; on the misty arms of the sea borne.

Ten Poems

1

Friend, out at the sea-south:
fixed in your time of year, how should you know me?
and have not even seen my mistress -
herself, though bodily near, else how far removed -
or my own eyes, How should you look
through the hot misty banks
where your Gulf sports on the meet of it, this north shore -
seeing from one, in wonder, to what is this other?

2

Land, when I look for land, for home, and no home see:
I look on your mountains, and find a place
that has lost even its name, in which all is a
waste of levels where plunge out, eye. So my homeland is out.
Yet I am in this place, which is not mine, happy -
that's put to sea and shrinks its bossed plain;
this buckle-rock not failing though fallen under swell
and gone in flood. It comes amazing sight,
this prick-bubble; so that I gaze
over sea and must be hard
within my blood's soft land against this land not mine,
hurting, this splinter to sight. For who has this has too much;

has the sheer beautiful country too near
when fanged, in mobile lipping seas, the breaker-rock country point
land looks. He in storms is held in the mouth,
in the eyes, in gale kissed.

3

These I went down, dumb; the lights are downed, for the motor
half-charged – heart, heart, like your falling – and then was shut down.
Till the ferry swung out
and I felt the fresh wind like a gust of pain past breaking,
like a stabbing breath, yet breathless:
the sudden filling of blood.
Then I had had crossed to the other land and felt the last wind;
yet I could not forget.

4

Now my hands
under your breasts,
full of kisses, are as under dark
the lightning;

which makes the cones
of pine tremble
which find the narrow
vivid boughs - your young arms
having love in them like the press of a May
leaf-sweet, sharp but a

green brazier flame, your bough of kisses.

By night
you are like a fine light of faggots,
the white willow has taken fire.
The shoots of the ash
are in your hands
for spring-thunder, come,
come as lightning,
come against my eyes like burning.

5
Women, you walk under the margin of
the reedy airlake, where he, having
caught, guessed, geared at it, now trembles.
Look up, in the humming heat.
The noon, like you, stands still without thinking,
or faintly drifts, as if past a glass which your breath might change,
or the finned pilot.
And there he hangs on safety invisibly, on a fraction of
four to five, and that narrow marginal
rush of airflood
in a whistling sphere, desperate
clutched, caught at, yet buoys him.
But the web of crystal braced air will fall, and he out of his will
down, down and if fall, the soft creature will down on you and through
fall; will losing, and motion and all but your cry at drowning.
You, hushed, will stand still, wait for the falling a long way
off; one hand to your mouth.
But the fraction will crash from four or five
in thinking drawing-offices, in the evening,
in the papers.

6
So he died, and the traction of the
engaging of gears, their grudging,
instantly – day then was night -
was changed. The spirit which had been so handsome in his eyes
fell out, a cheat,
leave him fie but as if sharped;
as if death had taken them for ransom.

7
What's death?
it's to forget

> that the gull flies up
> and the heron; by night the water follows their flight,
> crying, and the geese cry.

What? quickly
to lose

the birds fallen, fallen in a clot over the heart, where the
blood, runner, then dies.

What's death? that at autumn the light goes south.

8
Silence you yet remember to have been supple as a
reed in the air; when fleshly or fibrous
and long brilliant flowered now leans out of the gunpits
no silence. No silence. Here puts out his fronds death,
out of the blind his lovely corruption,
whose roots your shoulders pushed up
heavily when the gunsprings are fatigued; whose blossoms
are vivid death. And death purses his
whistling lips to breathe
his gathered honey sweet,
the sweet flowertubes of the trembling involved
firing-void in the air. He has put out those
pithed piping stems and shrilly
sucked deep, at Tannenberg; and the leaning flower
lateblown on that marsh-blue, naked, the gymnosperm,
has blown from its pistol in Sarajevo
to gunthunder at Quentin. Now is the death
a hollow in the air, barely put out.

9
This way we fell back
from pitch to pitched ambush, breathless, with the flight of the moon thrown up from
the metal. We skirted the arches, unloaded in Cates,
and each time the gun in the hand jumped again. Afterwards some fell back
under a wall
where that tongue's single instant end of death
in the barrel-spark and spoke to them, but they were already gone.

10
Though this year will go out,
yet it will have have been glad: with frost,
or summer's Adriatic gay, and enjoyed spring.
And that only so will pleasure come, morselled, instant,
accidental in the same orgasm; yet gay;
though the glowing lowers in the bowl
and the pipe not sweetens, nor the music.

HER EYES (FOUR POEMS)

1
The boats put out:
o put out hope
to follow over the water
the dear corrupt eyes
and hand of her my love, my love,
who fears my hands.
Away and down this river put
which, hers, to the stormless gulf
and landlocked flats of water
is running, where the vicious
salt-warmth of kisses may open her mouth.
Hers whose hands are tender for me yet cannot touch,
whose eyes go from my eyes to my mistress's.

2
Friend, when we spoke of her,
how true was that?
You know her to be dear, my dear;
I'll tell you how dear --
so that her sweet corrupt eyes follow me by day,
the hands which cannot touch me I touch tangibly at night,
friend. You said,
"She will sweeten":
yes, but not my mouth;
my pain will not give her
that pain she asks.
Friend, is this bitter? Think,
it is said for her who'd be mine yet cannot.

3
Nothing I may think of her, changing,
so can change my grief for her
as did her dear voice and corrupt eyes
when they said "Changeless, changeless,"
that day, in the changed light by the water.

4
Look on her, night: who, though away,
beautiful compels me as another night
to think of her bitterly,
of nights, waking which taught her corruption.
O, "Look," I said,
but so that look not
on the sweet, my sweet's hour sinning.
But wait; happy to look in her sleep afterwards
with a dream that she loves me;
and then, night, look to give her that dream,
which to her, lonely who cannot love, were dear,
were a glad gift of the night she has not had
and is not to have.
Give her my look, night.

Her Grief

Her eyes
trembling so with tears,
all her body hard she held
from the mercy of that plashing shuddering.
Then spirits of queens
seemed where she sat,
and thus the luxurious women of Rome awaited pleasure,
as she grief waited.
I would have put out my hand
and cried: "Spill now
the pearl-dissolving eyes their terror,
your fierce sorrow's body" --
but that had before called in our pleasure;
no words had I now hers,
and could not touch her.

Europe

Spring, the recession of water,
which turbulent sucked away under the land,
returns; but now in flood, higher than any main.
Now the blunt peninsula of Europe
noses into trouble;
not only flood, but floes shoulder up,
and the old glaciers like bears
wade out of the water.
Under, the rocks wait to be brunted again
with the parallel strokes of ice

and hibernation. We wait --
until garlands shall be frozen from the breath,
the blood will sift into the morains:
until at last the streams opening there
shall drain into the artery of the spring,
terrifying, its turbulence; sucking away the land.

CHAPTER 3

1931–1936 (Collected Poems)

Epithalamion

Now comes
that night which you cannot shorten:
which makes all else short,
and tentative makes those past days --
since first your look, under the eyes, was met,
or her frank look grew all at once grave;
until now, in the whitening room,
you said good-bye,
good-bye mother,
and to the sobered good friends
who fell shy quickly after the revel.

But those days, though growing shorter,
are not grown less, or less shy;
rather they are become different days,
now that, as in that look once,
the slow, grave night is declared.
She has bent her look again,
bend your head also a moment alone, in the garden --
knowing even that moment less long
than the long night is to be,
to its not known end:
whether tousled, bended eyes in the light,
or sleep, or a day which cannot be said.

Is it this her friends are saying?
whom you hear, with the likeness of voices,

S. Rennie (ed.), *Jacob Bronowski: Selected Poems*,
https://doi.org/10.1007/978-3-032-19597-5_3

behind the one light,
shaking her hair,
or with the likeness of the touch of hands.
O friends, young men, as you lead her,
lead him also;
that after the past days
which were so far together, capable,
he may learn to take her once
with no knowledge, but that she also is led;
and, silent, may take joy.

For it is joy to be taken to her;
joy is her gift --
to whomever she was given, knows that:
whether her father,
though he renounced it, for she was a gift to youth;
or youth, which now is rendering her.
Her raise joyfully, maidens
and speak her a last time with gifts;
for she leaves your speaking
at last when the one light is doused.
She hopes, longer than youth, for the still speech of two,
the dreamed after-talk of longing;
or matrons', or child's sayings; or always shy words.

Such words she will not wake from;
as she is unwoken now from her school's first words, or games --
although she let fall that sash
on that tunic long ago,
and only remembers them gratefully;
remembers the blush, and loved teacher.
Then raise those stuffs, and whisper
that no such showers any more, nor muslin,
shall cover her, girls,
with folds of a faint, long time;
when she dreamed, but did not dream of a prince.

And youths, whom he sought then in a dream,
not as needful, but as his need,
speak to him now of how he dreamed, alone,
and with a stumbling speech sought to say it;
rowing below the wood, or at night.
He tried to speak, he cried on silence
with a choked voice,
and the tears welled his throat,
and, unspeakably lonely, he stared up

alone, trying to say, "Can a word be understood ever,
whether I say it now, whether I cannot say?"

He shall say nothing now;
but softly you, youths, shall disclose to him,
and you, maidens, recall to her
days of hers he has not known:
her first days;
the young days when, with her fishing-lines,
out of the still, glintless
entanglements of sleep she climbed.
The early light hung on her
as upon dawn; as on her hair, girls,
the touch of your fingers now is lingering.

She climbed in the frosty sun
to the snow-pool under the distant, white, charmed mountain;
upon the fine carried lines her thoughts hung,
but untangled, untaken were as the pike
which, though held, though played and losing,
struck away and, suddenly sinking,
somehow was free.
The rod then dropped to her lap,
and her free thoughts, icy, are undiscoverable,
which sank; as under water
the mountain under the snow-cold stones sinks.

Like water,
her thoughts lapped on those stones,
knowing each by name
and to each giving a life.
Speak again those names to her, girls,
and softly his name,
that all be fine as the names of grasses or clouds for her
and all be as powerful.
For names spoke always in her thought,
her without a thought of power:
by names she sought, shining, confident,
to hold a whole to her,
as the tarn, imaging, sucks the sharp distant mount under.

Boys, you have seen her thus
from afar, when she was more and more alone:
she walked in her thoughts.
But he, who had first been lonely,
now spoke, singing, among you.
What was it his voice sought here --
which was neither grace nor company?

He sought power,
either to conjure again that one, unsaid speech;
or over you, youths, who had failed then to be spoken to;
who to-night in the garden speak back to him
and he listens, and trees and grasses
make your voices which he can call by no names.

For he knew those names
also that he might have power,
over trees, or the stream he named,
or the harsh master, and the dunce
whom a nick-name held in power --
and as the ravished secret of a name
then seemed to give knowledge of women.
But he, aware, putting out hands for power,
thereby escaped not the power of others;
while none could be powerful over her,
nor when she climbed, maidens, was it this she climbed away from.

She climbed from sleep;
though now you show her that
like a smoothing of the lines
which the pool had dragged back, involved, impossible.
For then her fingers on the line
began to tremble at a change;
not which was, but which might be;
of friendship to love. Love, friendship --
she was not yet taken, yet was no longer free upon the line;
and her fingers, a first time, thoughtless,
took pleasure in the ravelling.

Friendship, she thought, is like snow,
opaque, lazy, gracious to the mountain;
yet in the lucid moments of ice
arrogant also, and absorbing it.
But the poor love, outward though intense,
in the spring-pitted drifts sucks like water;
which shallowly takes the mountain-image
and the pinnacle down presses, powerless,
for self-sweeter pain.
Her touch wanted pain no more than power;
maidens, praise her ways
and always steady, unclosing hands.

Youths, urge his song,
which has already surpassed power
and faster presses, though no deeper
grows his voice, nor grows more thoughtful.

His thinking was so much later than hers,
and he had no such trouble of friendship;
but after the one silence
long kept his heart its silence,
unknown to him.
Onward his song then learned nothing but knowledge:
capably to run in lanes; and, though purposeless, to have a goal.

When to learn was, to be companionable;
his dilatory pleasure in his lab was, to know.
She too, girls, then in learning
took your hands; yet broke blindly the ring,
ungoverned, shy, for this or that knowledge.
While wakeful he seemed to run;
but the field, glassy, reasonable, was entranced,
which logic witched, which was a shaven nature.
She stumbled still through dreams: not or a prince;
yet hesitant; growing to know famous names.

Boys, now take hands, and girls,
and a moment fearful walk together
of a change in her dream
or his changing knowledge.
For now first they saw one another --
but with unregarding eyes
and they knew not the future.
Or could it have been that she knew?
that the silent fear then began upon her heart,
which brooded, mountainous, prophetic,
and like, the white over the water;
unravelling at once away from father-lines the single self-line?

What she feared was she -- knew not what.
It was not pain,
but an invisible, louring dread to come:
nameless, it was the one unfulfilled pain.
By her helpless threads to her mother then
she seemed to give it a name,
and pain of childbirth thought
what was inexpressible dread;
which not even the mountain's hurt and fear,
though not far now, though growing, could surpass.

Again out of sleep she climbed then
upstream to the rubbled glacier bed,
where fear might be forgotten
and that inner piercing, peaked dread; yet growing, yet growing.
She cast her fly, and suddenly the line leaped,

and running out over the spool took, caught her up:
her gay as if with the fish, and free, though against him,
running; her blood like the river-clear over stones ran.
The mountain-white or green struck her down
out of her dream and secret life,
and the running spool was as a light unhidden:
prince, he had a first name,
he stood in the eye in amazing incognito.

That brilliant, blinded moment,
youths, you cannot imagine,
who see it only like lightning burning under the horizon.
There it is vivid and alive.
But in her it withered the dread
and her dream at once; and her eyes were staring.
Where she stood the stream had narrowed
and the dangerous climb above the morain hung over:
here comes no fish's striking
or mountain-image, to take the short breath;
and the line runs vainly. Maidens, then she knew
her shall no more that movement move.

How quiet it has grown:
almost the voices beyond the light are hushed;
the insistent voices in the garden are low,
youths, are yours. And low they tell
that now the shadow of a mountain dilated his eyes.
Green and rock were a wonder to him,
they became a passion;
and the abrupt sun rising over the arête
struck his heart, struck from his heart its silence.
Youths, who touch her tresses, belayed his rope
at the traverse, or the dangerous step-crossing in the sun:
you saw, here he lived; he was jubilant and still

Thus him also the mountainous moment overbore
once or twice; and enormous moved --
but not as she had been moved. For neither ben nor alp,
nor dropping under sail below the sound,
so deadly could move, to a dazzled close,
him whom her dread had not darkened
nor her fierce shut courage.
When suddenly the air ran for him as a river,
as a glacial wild side piled, or falls, or night,
he breathless remembered the moment he had tried to speak,
nostalgic which yet cried: but he was content.
And the air thickened, mist was on the fells;
there she had learned to be brave, to walk delicate and lively.

She was awake;
and he out of his undreaming
but nightmare youth walked: he saw more clearly.
Yet when he saw her again, all at once,
he was bewildered.
to be falling silent,
to speak anew and strangely
and to one so gentle.
Then he knew himself for what he was --
one unlearning that he has been a learner;
learning to be alone. She still stared at him,
but in her eyes began honour and a kind of marvel.

And here sounded upon her
your song, maidens: you drew to her
stuffs, and showed her shops.
In place of the fishing at dawn
you pressed on her tenderness, and an unshaped hope:
not wholly to be his, yet as if for him.
And him, astonished, you made aware
of his trivial days, sailing, reading, or at college;
penitent made him of delight which, lightly,
strings days into a life.
You showed him the future upon her eyes, grave as a glass.

So has he grown
to look steadily at the present,
which to-night in the garden
at last he lifts his head to --
and a moment must your voices cease,
boys and girls; though singing you shall return.
He must think, not without great bitterness,
of the many time she stood thus before,
irresolute, yet resolved.
Who did he fear? This moment. He fears it.

Garlanded maidens, return from her, the certain one;
and, youths, speak among the laurels: tell him,
this should have troubled him as a boy;
but to-night to him, older than that,
beautiful shall she come,
and beautiful always be,
the bride to the groom's passionate hands;
he beautiful shall not be apart, yet tremble to be closer.

Thus shall be repaid
to her the named dread, childbirth.
And fear and dread shall be fruitful to them;

the recent days, leaning together in the grass,
of eye-shut sun-red, followed by red harvest sun,
when dread grew less, the inner piercing
peaked sweetness mounted, yet lingering was as a dread --
all past, shall bear fruit.
If in a year comes her bursting pain,
it will have ripened more than nine months.

Now your voices have recanted,
youths, his last regrets:
softly sing, and let him think
how she rises, and the silver bodice falls.
And now what was dreamed is real;
what in sunred, certain days
seemed knowledge of one another,
when indeed little was to be known, yet which seemed rich --
richer it grows than ever before,
but is hesitant.
He knows how much is hidden, that he must reach to-night.

Richer what was before? ask him, youths --
among shops, or her games,
your beginning gift: what riches
can he say? Yet he thought all rich.
Then, you young, deny him.
You, maidens, sing, not rich but gentle,
gentle were her days, she is come dearly
through the speech of maids
and their later garden games, is come
Those days made her still worth, long hence shall enrich day.

Then you made for her voices,
that his voice be a deep bell, or water;
your touch had tender been
that, in brightness lying,
he as the light strike.
in a shocked flow, flame-sweet;
and in your gardens
she had once, as if by later day,
that dark-still in which now,
alone, he will seek her. Tell him, maidens.

Yours were the voices which came
and went from her, late,
for that voice, not his, but as his; royal.
Now a last time they are loud; you sing.
Your touch did not move, nor his, but as his,
the dreamed prince's.

Now for a last time
it folds away the gauze skirt,
that the tender thighs be for touch,
not prince's, but his, the lover's.
Out of the garden let him come, and dark, still to her.

And unfold the bed, maidens;
youths, prepare him to the door,
on whom the night, as on a future day, is grave.
Show him the post,
her the fall of dark, moving, beyond the door;
which now shut. Lift about her the curtained
cold bed-dark, for the touch-warm, voice-warm night.
Lift, youths, his eyes
and her bent look, maidens:
let them see once that all is the seeing;
before touching to see, blind,
and after touch nothing more seeing, nothing felt.

CRISIS

(...You come to this town, as no multitude
of angels, or judges, but some men who'd
see; not gloss Evil, or yet scamp good.)

Parade then, many, and you few, review
Virtue. Item, to be new.
Item, now to be industrious;
when the spasm dies, to cut the loss.
To have, to hold - a credit? or what
asset? a pedant or two who'll not
confess his lost helplessness when the end
hammers on gates, refuge is not with friends.

So, item, to live; that's no holiday
When there's a death abroad, a decay
at home. Item, yet to have learning:
for that's their skill, on learned earning
to live – they are to two cities each are
a thousand warnings, vividly to teach
ten thousand to stay fools and grow the richer.

Say therefore, item, to recompense
the knowers with knowledge; the knowing, with better sense.
Give to the potent, privilege; to the poor
their insured benefits; as, bonus in the future;
ignorance or night-schools; whorishness or prudery;

all impudent forced choices - but of family!
Item, give in marriage: the bad stock
to the profligate, the drab, to the anaemic;
he, who has nice hair, call him pervert,
shove him on a duchess and let him learn to love.

But who writes good verse, call him savage. Item,
the obscure livers
cry to him that lights them
"O most outer darkness" if not "Bogey!"
cry and the hunt's up: parson, pimp and fogey,
those hard riders, are holloa-ing; while from the brush-wood
the critic breathes "There, but for the grace of God –"

O graceful God, thou nimble over fences
where long have hung thy elect's more stubborn pants,
thou who the needy givest at once his tabloid
cross and drug: the dean, Stopes and his adenoid;
the hound givest, God, good fox, and better bitch,
Hitler his Jew and Lewis: which is which?
Art thou an item, God? or art thou too
a bank's intangible credit, a taboo
of exchanges, hush in the City?
(rumour it, assert it, sit on in committee)?
God, if you're not an item - you're a pity!

But, few, leave joking; you see the sharp ferment
rise: item last, a nation's government.
O no lame, no fumblers; the picked of three
sides are nothing if not good company.
from one the shoddy and the boor, he
with hardened arteries; from one, the crafty;
one, humdrum and bigot, and the arrogant. Fools
who rule by right, for rightness find by rules,
whose power is posture, a rhetoric intent
powerless to husband, to foresee, prevent
to act. This item of limping on the event
aging and bankrupt men, that have no quality
even of courage, meets bankruptcy
with the self-righteous broadcastings of hope.
Meeters of an end with twaddle; eyes, with dope.

Yet, retch at these, be grateful; they are the small
fry! There's to stomach the powerful,
the speculators and oilfinders, the
racketeers; the armament royalty.
After the mean men, these certain ones; but
think them not magnificent or desperate,
or big; they're the sneak absentees, who win.

Whom will you swallow, whom reject? the not mean
yet pin-eyed, the insane? chew politic
Lady Astor, or spew (the late) Joynson Hicks
Builders of conscience on squint and
see, the clouds buckle, squinting lies a land.
Rich squints to rich, and Sodom; poor, to Rome,
with whom squints aesthete, ass; and who squints home
but that boiled egg Columbus taught to stand
(dissemble cock)? He droops now, but not the hand
of God from Oxford, for when godly who sees
Sitwell and Mosley go halves in a codpiece.

Squint are their eyes, their hands, the squint ears
have wagged "Tariff" or "Free Trade" thirty years,
squint yet they mouthe it; or "Gold" or "Inflation"
while the wind rises, that is no nation's
wind, the sudden, final, unbelieved; a
wind blowing the bibles through Geneva.
While praise the pilot, Garvins - this week that
he saved the pound; next, that he let it smack.
While praise God, all for what? for being skinned,
for being alive; for fun; and I, for wind.

STORY

Stories slide hardly through
the sticky mind, now
that the pigment blood
stiffens with the falsehoods
which have reddened sleep, and the heart pumping
and cheeks. More seldom the wind
blows immediate, unregarded, past
the eyes in thought or the fast
fixed mouth-frown, so that the mouth kisses,
the river freshening at once is
through them, and the stories ask
"What have I done?" - felt, and made stark
bodily movements; but it was no sham ageing
first put my young hands from moving.
Stories did it, yet their rich clutter
made me myself and not another.

Be it a story then of her
who had the kiss and seemed near
in the wind, the river-silver.
If, when she was born, I shivered,
I do not remember, nor her youth;

but when I saw her, my mouth
moved. Love may be such an unclasping
of thought, and sensible seeing.

Then did truer see her
in a dream in Wales, or where
we for days together climbed over the
unbelievably irreal snowfields, rock-arêtes? If gusty
this should have been, whereas that might
story-still lie, it was not right:
yet stories were lost in it when morains and
drain of river-white at night put mine into her hand.

After, indeed, the dream's
shocking precision in her gestures seemed
to show her with the pleasure of recognition
when returned: but the vision
of goddesses, Rome, stories, though there,
fell away under the real dreaming body-stare.

And after and after, making now, what moil
of wind and fable, clotting, have coiled
in one blood; and swirl of rock and water lacing,
jutting into one another, given her foam face
what player queen's death-look,
what flint, sharply struck
spurt? I do not know. Whether
the rivers now run, or stories, they're hers.

And it may be her doing, that not sense
nor either of these two violences
fills me; that she is the fine
balance of what is beyond my mind
or my body: knowledge
that I stand on my world's edge.

STARING

I have not greeded
happiness, or my ends;
but been for friends'
and lover's need,

that they their desperateness
might tell at night.
The lines under my eyes
I put to dazzling restless

astrology for these,
and to the magic she
asked. Now always,
out of the mirror or
crystal, lost pleasure
stares back terribly at me.

Revenge

REVENGE. - One Carpenter, of Bicester, in Oxfordshire, drowned himself in
a pond, to be revenged of one Aldworth, who held an annuity of 30 *l.* on his life,
but who had offended him by calling him by an opprobious name. - *True Sun.*
                                        The Times, 27th March, 1832.

1
Poet and geometer,
I read with pride Socrates's
praise of the two arts;
and, man, am arrogant that he's
spoken proudly of men:
that they wrong but in
the mistaking of rightness.

Poet and man, I read
haughtily how Bruno held his
truth highly, and
Galileo made no peace
but with Italian, exact passion;
geometer, take joy, that fashioned
Segre our art of the faith of these.

Man and geometer, I
read truth to be a fineness
made greater than nobility; and, poet,
that the adherence to truth is
no faculty, but is the soul
in singleness, and in being whole:
poet, man, geometer, I am headstrong in this.

2
But the generation of the zealous
does not survive;
which, poet, has thrown me here
like flotsam, wave-alive

but inanimate, a spar
of its wrecked jammer;

those who read a course for that
were fine geometers

with as great ones to man
what now's no ship more,
but a fluid motion on the shore,
leaving the ebb ribbed, deathly clear.

3
Thinking thus, I read
of a foolish man who is dead -
and died with me, we drowned together,
being tired, looking at the weather
of politics and finance;
foolish, wilful, askance
men, we wearied of being called
cuckold of the glib world
or loony by sane times,
bastard of their climate.
He was the wittier,
to take of financiers
moneyed revenge; for I who seem
more generous in unrevenging, blame
myself, that I bring no fierceness
to have of them redress.
Therefore I honour him, sorry
Carpenter, whom a stupid quarrel
gave a glimpse of fury, so that he'd seen
a moment the submerged moon
uncoined, the night ghost of
its wrecked ship bullion-proof:
upon the unsteady water of the time he put his heel,
and, as it slid away, slipped after the phantom keel.

Thus he drowned himself, whom one Aldworth,
that on his life had some money's worth
of annuity, had in the round
farmer safety of that bond
called a scurrilous name.
A silly story, and a lame
crazy revenge; yet does its callow
figment kindle suddenly the tallow
time, I see the half mad,
half bitter gesture of the drowning man;
the decision of his wild mind
in certain revenge is fine
in my geometer's imagination;
as the true, whole folly is in

the poet's, and all that resolute and abused sense
is accepted, arrogant in the man's.
I see the drowning man make
with the moon image on the lake
a moment's frenzied company: then go down.
I see the last moon-struck age drown.

4
That farcical show having been enacted, is dismissed:
he who was called, who knows, gallowsbird, atheist,
is with him who was, maybe, crooked and both.
Their ghosts make little bicker now of the truth.
Only I am left here to take no heart of that,
fixed upon the time grown podgy with profit.
None of it I arraign, I look but
into those past generations of my heart,
then passionately I look out from them:
poet, man, geometer and proud of them.

The Sensual Law

Awake, I sometimes speak;
but sleep is a government matter --
Hush, which His Grace's minister issues
with the initials of angels: the command
"Submit! you too long
withstood the sensual law."

"Jubilee! Jubilee!"
then sings the benign night
which flutters from throne to throne:
down Jacob's shiny ladder,
on which is spitted the dove Regina,
and each smiles very white "Amnesty!
See how trivial was
your heady treason, sabotin.

"And all are joyful
that you repent.
And forgive you, with double beds
for sureties,
that thereby be yours, most dear brand,
the privilege of lawful dreams. --
Compliments of Colonel Lynch:
Couple with that soft assurance.

"To sleep you strained
your sandy throat,
what did you cry?
That rather you had pitched, face-first,
in that crownland
dune and dune of nightmare
which sleepwalkers maze in?

"No, rebel, the flesh grants
no such vainglory
to a daily defeated intellect.
You claimed justice
like a calculating head.
Justice also the sense administers,
no Devil's Island of which
but numbered to the sleeper are
its drugging grains of sand.
Bedded therefore, your desert,
forget your petty mutiny."

My Eyes

At the harsh front
of my eyes stand
two images: hers, and
my own, there brunt
against each other, one
thrown inward by her light,
and mine by my sight
out flung in a sharp cone.
They threaten together with arms
a pin-trick will show,
but they are alive, though shadow,
and the grotesque harms
of their battle are my mind's,
which seems to give each its
gestures, to each reaches
out blood for wounds.
Yet all is only seen; there are no sounds.

The mimic fight with its
frontier on my lids
clashes ghastly in the double light,
so still, as is by night
the breath, and unknown to touching.
Not my brain or hers could bring
that forth; and we

thus aghast see the frenzy,
I cry out, and I hear her cry
"Whose are these phantoms? Why
do lovers meet with visors
grinning, and gaping hate's eyes?"

At the cry, the field is
bare as if by cock-crow, there are no lists.
We put out our hands, there is nothing
but the fine touch which we, loving,
always had. We are together, and say
"The dead must have come in broad day
with enmity against us both. Where
plucked they such hatred from the air?"

It was not air, or mind
of one or other was unkind.
It came by sight. The glassy sense
flung it to and fro in a lens
that seared her image in my eye
and thrust mine outward as fiercely,
and each and each pressed on
the film of seeing like a burn.
Love is no sense: for that
tugs all to wilful
bellied distortion like a crystal,
and doubles for fantastic hate
with the sense's mock stereoscope
two visions of the single love.
Love is no sense: but if
love lodges in
the senses, it is refined
at the junction of all five
to unison in the mind.
We, certain of being one,
can know it in them all alive.
but in each sense it dies, and haunts
it with a ghostly, echoed taunting.

Love is no sense, but deeply
sits where the sense sleeps,
where locked are eyes and
breath and hands,
and even mind stills
its steam, that's fired by all
their tindery or glowing coal.
Only the urgent yet still
order wakes there, the one; and will

hold us to be one.
Love is awake, the fulfilled,
the single, and not done.

HOMER IS MY EXAMPLE

Those heavy-jowled poets, Goethe, Yeats,
lay late, plunging with women. When
they rose, stupid, the brilliant light
struck from their drugged eyes anew night
lightnings. Drunken, prophetic, they
fabled from sleep to snoring sleep
with mouths flushed at women's teats.

In age they kept the medlar-sweet
wisdom sucked there. Their turbulent lips
fell to a trembling steadiness
more stubborn speaking, but not less
soft-cored, that fumy frenzied verse;
not now Sibyl-riddled in abandon,
but stony, hollowed as her seat.

I woke too early, when my taste
had not that gross night-nurture,
nor such a tasty wisdom drew
I from the freezing daybreak dew.
Bone-cold then truth grazed me, which
rolled soul and bumpy skull to rounds:
but had no air, or handsome waist,

and no delighting mouth -- nor I
have a mouth in kissing o's
dissolved to sob the pleasure death.
Truth presses with a sharper breath
upon this glass, this verse. It frosts
no nodding garden, starry, there,
but figure of a measured die.

I as the instrument take pride
in surer than the oracular speech
of those poets, Goethe, Yeats,
the tranced, marvellous, medium cheats
at Delphi or a woman's breast,
Those temples are fallen, I
saw their blackened ruin lie:
I see nothing there, but truth beside.

CHRIST

He did not walk salt blood, nor the storm
of tears; and the nature he stilled, although
grosser than mine, was less sea-changed, less violent.

Nor Orpheus, whom panthers licked, hushed such
harsh cries as mine, shaking the animal throats.
More brute than theirs my senses break my speech.

Desire the sea and sense the beast goad me
to horror: but the horror is not made by them.
Thought is the fine point which pricks to agony.

Thought of you is agony by day, thought of
myself sets horror hunting at night.
Then the sea flood at the moon, and the beasts

come to the salt-licks with blood on their tongue.
Thought is the master of the pack; I run before it
like Orpheus not looking back, like Christ

the moon-struck walking the roofs of water.
I dare not call out to me lest I fall.

CRISEYDE

That bitten, wanton flesh, Criseyde's,
which had put her heart to shame,
maybe was not to be blamed.
It was her mind which was afraid

that words lover once spoke may hiss
so long, that the eager ear grows deaf:
then the flesh no lover chafes
suddenly shivers, and the unkissed

eyes stare wildly back at eyes
an old, lonely woman rolls.
How could Criseyde, how can I know
whether the mind, which fears this, lies?

I gamble my peace of heart on words
my heart holds like a shell; though she
who once spoke them be now gone, be
kind or dead; they cannot be unheard.

If mind bade her flesh lie warm
some nights, I am not proud to lie
cold because I hear that cry
she feared, and think I take no harm.

Maybe I fear my flesh's, as she
feared her mind's nightmare: I shrink
the leper touch she did not think
to fear. Criseyde, Criseyde, maybe

she knew how soon her shining eyes
kisses would make leper blind;
and chose to be blind, rather than the mind's
frenzy, the shell of the heart's cries.

I lie cold because I choose,
and she chose to lie warm.
If she felt no blame, or qualm,
it is not I who can accuse.

We Hold Our Breath

We hold our breath when we are told
the story of the field of gold.

Glory of princes is a tale
the hundred years do not stale.

The frantic crowd that cheers it hoarse
marched with broken throats from wars.

Bitten lung and bloody crown
came on crutches then to town.

Tattered garlands hung the loins
of them whom gunshot left no groins.

Does the bedded king remark
their nightmare army after dark?

And with a little cough set down
the bloody sceptre and the crown?

Does he listen to the dead
riding the bombers overhead?

The shadow of another war
walks with armoured cars before.

He does not shiver in whose lap
a cloud of gas rolls up the map.

　　......

He knows and he does not quail
whom the stricken cities hail,

about whom dead men crowd and sing.
He lifts his head and is a king.

1937–1940 (Collected Poems)

Two Valentines

Spring bursts his rockets through the branches,
and throws the couples to the ground;
over their locked eyes
he sets the buds flaring.

And on lovers walking alone
he drops, like Danae's,
his golden shower.

......

The slow sap beats a drum:
then the swallow's wings tremble,

and the girl hears a gale in her ears,
and the boy stands still;

looking at one another.
Louder than drums
the lovers fight for breath.

The Gangster

The gangster with the sawed-off gun
straddles the sea. There, under glass

© The Author(s), under exclusive license to Springer Nature
Switzerland AG 2026
S. Rennie (ed.), *Jacob Bronowski: Selected Poems*,
https://doi.org/10.1007/978-3-032-19597-5_4

film-fan and man-of-war lie still.
His emblematic armour has overwhelmed them,

his visored face. The plume of smoke
nods in his hand like welcome, death
to those whom it delights. The dark
dazzles them with pleasure whom the gun-play thrills.

But through the screen his hand has picked
his trigger-men from them, and set
them drumming in bombers over Spain.
The Moor and the Stormtrooper are his legion.

The Jew and Georgian obey him,
and, sick, the Pope who cries against
them 'Anti-Christ'. Their words glow in
the bivouacs, and the children see them

touch off the beaconed hills, it's war!
Who will not clap his hands when these
fanatics, and the strong-arm men,
burst their ripe rockets on the zero hour?

Who will gainsay them, who has sat
at dark, and thrilled to see the moll
nestle a gun in furs? The spool
spins in a maze of silk, smoothly; and then

the news-reel of the shell-struck church
and broken tree hums. And the gangster
straddles the screen; there, under gas,
film-fan, man-of-war, and a world adore him.

THE SLEEPING AND THE DEAD

Under your hunch-backed shadow, man,
stoop: and lift the candle higher.
The eyes of portraits do not shine
like fuses. And the fired
nerve does not burn to mines
under the ancestral faces. Man,
you do not fright the dead. And when
the wainscot blazes, they remain.

The gallery runs into dark.
Look closer. These are unborn. What train

of powder will you lay, to shake
the snoring foetus and
the ungot unawake?
Put up your fire, man. You'll not make
the future wise because you scorch
your fingers at the foolish torches.

Out of your eyes into your eyes look,
man. The sleeping and the dead
are but as pictures there. Fantastic
in your garish light
of match and dynamite
they stand; and all the shaken mind,
the burning head and blind,
are yours. Lift up your candle, man, and shine
it in your eyes, or blow a world to ruin.

Take Your Gun

Man, take your gun: and put to shame
earthquake and plague, the acts of God.
You maim the crazy and the lame.

Terror is their palsy, the knees
of men buckle for fear of man.
You are the God whom frenzy pleases.

You are the gas-man, and the flier
who drops his bomb; the man in tanks.
You wire mines and fear the fire.

And dig the hollow street with trenches
the gas-main and the sewer cross.
The stench of dead men makes you flinch.

But, if the dying whimper, pain
pricks you like courage, like delight.
The vein sings to the cruel brain.

What are you, man, that gun in hand
with savagery and pity go,
and face to face with madness stand;

and acid-drenched and poison-sprayed
see flame run lovely like a wake

from raiders; and the burning lake
shake overhead? You are afraid.

The shadow flickers on the wall
like morse, like gun-shot. Terror walks
the tall roofs where the snipers hawk.
He stalks you, man. And, man, you fall.

SPAIN *1939: FOUR POEMS*

GUADALAJARA

March-weather storms the house like shrapnel.
I hear the ice roar, and the guns.
And in the silent, sentry passes
the crazy dead stand to attention.

What did Napoleon see, who stared
at Moscow as I watch the fire?
Frost climbed the window-pane for him,
but for his men the snow piled higher.

And Hannibal in the Alps, did he
rage at the cold and blame his luck?
The elephants and soldiers did
not listen as they froze to muck.

Caesar with Spanish slingers shivered
in Gaul; but knew the beds at home
would yet be warm. The slingers died.
And Caesar - Caesar whored in Rome.

In Libya the shaken sword
aches in the sun. The conquering boor
sweats and grows hoarse. But here his men
cough death beside the dying Moors.

What shall the rigid soldier say
who knows the cheat, yet cannot turn?
The ice builds bayonets in his veins
and the rough frost like anger burns,

and pity plucks him by the sleeve
and whispers in his ear that kings
will still be snug when water runs
the courses of his blood in spring.

What is my pity worth? I fret
no frozen body, but my mind;
and if I tremble, all my rage
weighs nothing in the bite of wind.

Forgive me, men at posts, who stiffen
for furies such as kings' or mine;
and suffer me no more than speak
the words your lips will never form,

the hope that hangs there like a breath
that fate shall break your frozen line,
break kings and break fanatic men;
that March shall break the world with storm.

THE DEATH OF GARCIA LORCA

Step after step into the darkened landscape
we mourners walk with you: until the guns speak.
Speak to the muffled dead for the loss
of the gipsy's glory and the matador's.
Walking, did you see the cape and the dancers
flutter and fall still, the falling lances?
The picador is Don Quixote,
the gipsy begs, and the poet's
mouth is bloody. Blood reddens
the windmill arms of Armageddon.
O this is your end, your end, your end;
the sails say it. Call to your friend
or the gunman, but neither is with those
you loved: the spendthrift, the mumming, the toreros.
None walked so far the roads of the tramps
and the singers to the gipsy camps,
and joked with the sharpers and dancers and whores
and the trick-riders and picadors.
You joked with the dead: did you not hear
their voices lower year by year?
their dumb trumpets? and the word Doom
when the gun's echo answered the drum?
You walked with ghosts, and their time is done.
Call to your friends, but we are one
with the gunmen then. Ours is the cause
of the grinding mill and the crowded house
and the men who walk between mill and home.
Our future is not easy come.
Step by step into the darkened country
we walk with you there; but the light gentry

walks no more, nor the gipsy kings.
And out of that dark the poet sings.

GREECE AND SPAIN

Greece closed the western world at Spain.
Beyond was hearsay. Unknown tides
plucked at that gate; the living failed.
The dead stood tense and open-eyed.

The fable sinks to oracle.
Did Delphi guess the western world
would pitch its end at last in Spain?
would break its gate; and high on furled

wings bring the dead, like locusts, where
the olive leaf had promised peace?
The bomber leaves a wilderness
to those who tried to make it Greece.

Athens foretold this: for it ended
like this. Like this the soldier dead
from Sparta came, the Persian hired
guns, against the men who lived

in peace. A burning countryside
ringed Pericles. He fell the first.
Then poor men starved; the rich man won.
The olive root of freedom burst.

Now round the Spanish coast the eyes,
like signals, of the dead are blazing.
But dark in trenches stand the men
they do not cow; whom not the treason

of captains, nor the priest in arms
bears down. The living stand. Roughly
and desperate at Madrid, they still
gainsay the locusts' prophecy;

and prove that freedom yet shall plant
a tree, a town, where once the west
closed Greece; and that the gate of Spain
opens the Islands of the Blest.

This is a Grecian story too:
there is a gate beyond defeat.

The fable ends in hope; the leaf
shall live, the locusts shall retreat.

BOMBER

This ruin, where you dropped the bomb,
was not a house: it was a home.
The body riddled by your gun
was not a soldier, but a man.
Nor was it death, but war, among
shattered olive-roots and dung,
which made the land the dead man wooed
with water to be cowed with blood;
an ooze from broken conduits, where
the desert walks back over-year.

Stranger above, this is your debt:
a soil, a fruit he made with sweat,
a farm he built. You shall not fly
the reckoning of the man who died.
Your life long you shall go in fear
of what his barren land will bear;
till, where you sowed with shot, you reap
the buried arms his children kept.

You gave to stone and cactus what
had been a soil: the ore shall not
forget you when it starts through these.
There shall be olives on the trees,
sons on the farm; the debt be paid,
though he who duns you was long dead.
Remember him the day your plane
falls in the fields which wanted rain,
You shall not murder them again.

BIRTHDAY ODE

Ice rounds the year
the spurred foot of the skater sounds on
with a grace which belies
the iron striking fire from ice,
iron spurting a flower --
sudden as your mind
fires and makes flower your eyes,

your smile;
and the sky
on the wide fen of your brow breaks
and your clouded look is bright.
The frozen meadow bursts.
Spring is your thought,
wherein the year begins.

Begins again when the heel
leans on the wind
and shears the grained ice,
making a rite of the ring of fire
to bring spring.

To give the lush, the knee-deep meadow
its steep of flood like sleep,
and then the light, warm
like your waking flush.
You stir to wake,
and take day unaware
and bring the summer slake.

Warm then walk the seasons
of your flesh.
Your mouth parts for the berry,
and the clover
to autumn reaches down,
over the meadow;
over the flushed leaf
heaves the wind in gusts,
that frost may bite
white through the parted lips.
The ice slips forward.

And the year is yours
full in a ring, in a cup
where the iron puts flowers.
The skater closes the figure:
the edged, the etched
fine as your mind
and sharp with white sedge, rounded.
Now the clouded ice rounds the year,
and grows bright in your look,
and your thought
cups seasons between eye and eye.

You Sought the Shadow

Familiar with the lion and gazelle,
your voice makes Africa a friend, whose whims,
whether gold or scrub, are gay and amiable;
who'll tease with fevers to deny a glimpse
of a river-source or a savage ceremonial;
and, smiling that the hero braves a hell,
will yield her monsters to the travel films.

All this, unsaid, is audible when you talk
easily of anything but your years of thirst
in deserts where the barefoot hunters walk;
nor do your words betray that you were first
betrayed when you believed this land might make
a life for you, that would not need to stalk
nostalgia in streets; but found it cursed.

You sought the shadow that the antelope
shakes in the sun; and what was vast and fine
in mountain spaces seemed to answer hope
that man might live so high, and yet combine
the homely with the climber's dream. That rope
was sand, the mountain desert: and when you dropped
you did not grovel for the golden mine.

Because you were mocked, your voice to-day makes mock,
friendly as Africa; as smooth, as bright;
nor is your secret less because you lock
your eyes and play conspirator with the light.
The arid plains are present in your look,
and all the continent that you forsook
lies like oppression on your secret sight.

Forget to mock, because you could mistake,
and put the whimsical friendship of that land
away. You have learned that the plains and the rocks were fake.
Count yourself fortunate to understand
the false nostalgia; and be free to make
a life unbound alike by streets and rock.
It is yours to build; and what you build can stand
when streets are desert and the lion sand.

God

God: more than man: more bitter, but more just:
forgive me, man: and be forgiven that

you made me this: but not my witness: not
that among less than men, than beasts, you thrust
me up to see and sicken, and share lust
with these: knee-deep in terror set, and hot
with murder splashed me, and sharp with shot:
and made me speak of this because I must.

Speak, among those who lie: and must, among
the wanton with the whip: you have bared my nerves
to years when striplings kill whom boys betray:
have shown me honor like the drug they crave.
You have made me witness what the madmen do:
make me not say it, God: God, strike me dumb.

VICTORY

Flood chokes the Ebro gorges. The golden orchards
strangle with blood. And to the coast, the guns
roll and scream. Rock and ricochet howl.
This is the desert, Spain.

Here lopes the snub-nosed bomber. The hyena
befriends the tank. By broken harbours dive
the plated fish, the torpedoes. And the ships
ooze their grain and sink.

Man stubborn in your shelter; who goes hungry
for death: who storms a ruin and is proud;
scratches a hole to hold a gun, until
his belly rips: soldier,

what do your guts dung? Not, lovely, the vines
in shattered valleys; or a monument
for kings; nor peace. Larger than these, which give
a landscape life, you die

to blast it. Poison is sweet to your breath
because it sours the soil, and makes corrupt
what kings still covet. And that a tyrant fail,
you welcome the wilderness.

Yes, in a heap of stones you have proved your choice.
Soldier, be comforted. Your wall will stand.
The land stands. You are the master, man.
And when the general lords it

down the dead Ebro reaches, he knows no ore
or furrow's his, though shot pile it head-high.
Fanatic man, glad of the cactus, be fine.
You have made a kingdom desert; but made it Spain.

Not All Lose Hope

Not all lose hope. The boy who ploughed
up muskets climbs somewhere the passes
of the Pyrenees, uncowed.

Proud, the Catalonian wrecks
his truck, to be an outlaw
and a beggar on the muleteer's tracks.

The Maxims have not overcome them.
who will light their signal-fires
from the coasts to Guadarrama;

whose rumour, like a sultry night,
will stand electric over wakeful
cities; till a landscape, bright

with lightning, knows their coming, like rain,
like peace. The starving yokels
shall share bread with them; and over Spain

again the guerrilleros raise
their salute: the surer than death,
the hunted, underground, victorious.
They kept their hope. They will keep faith.

The Death of Karl Kraus

Kraus died in time: before the God
he honoured as his equal, who shot
Lorca, and brutally smashed
Mühsam's delicate ears, washed
Vienna with his cleaning squads.

Now becomes God the anger which
Kraus spilled upon the dunged and rich
ferment Vienna. God also saw
the Danube spawn this medlar culture,
and plunged to drain it like a ditch.

Would Kraus to-night think it given
him as a grace, if he were driven
by boors to clean latrines? Or would
that bitter Jew pray for his God's
forgiveness, but would not forgive?

O yes, the age which he disowned
was easy, ageing, overblown.
Kraus prayed an age sharp as day
might etch his eyes: who, had he stayed,
would see an age like night come down,

and sharp and savagely blind
the poet's eyes, and splash his mind
bloody from a knacker's wall.
Hate and terror walk the malls.
Below the city, torture mines

the cellars, O Mühsam, Lorca,
I call to you across the dark
age, ere my voice too is dumb.
Give courage when the headsmen come.
Give to the desecrated God
whom Kraus unleashed, once more his manhood.
Give light where only ghosts, your ghosts are.

THE DEATH OF PIUS XI

Peace in his mouth, his heart death, goes
to God His chosen, the three-crowned Prince Pius.
In Spain, Moors say his Masses.

Arabs awe Jerusalem
with Roman guns: below whom
the Holy Sepulchre mourns its gem.

Attila, scourge of infidels,
scrawls crooked crosses on the walls
of Europe; and the Cardinals

flutter them from the towers he sacks.
The Beast of Revelation's tracks
score the eyes which break on "Pax".

Father, forgiving God the God
in you you suffered and defeated,
be you forgiven the life you lied,

and mock, and fear: what of the liar
in death? You blessed the bomber's fire
and, tall, the sniper in the spire,

that these be faithful and destroyed
men in Vienna, boys in Madrid,
witnessing charity unto God.

It is the dead must answer "Peace",
Pope, now that Attila, the Caesar
and dervish, cannot beg His pleasure?

Martyrs on the floor of jade
must hide their blood to-night, to plead
mercy for your grim crusade,

and for pity beg the good
you robbed with churches, from your God.
Pope, are you arrogant, taking grace,
a flower from the mouth of those
you wept for, and with peace struck dead?

The Bullfight

Astrologers and boxers with trumpets,
spangled, on plumed horses, are first. Strumpets
and dowagers to hounds, with sharpers
and provocateurs walk next. After
them free-lance and gigolos, child-stars
ride. And behind walk the angular
banderilleros in wigs, the pasty
bishops, the politicians. Last
come, lovely in their capes, the killers.

Three blasts
sound and all bow. The racketeers roar in a ring.
The procession breaks. And we wait to begin.

Wait the gentle, breathless, and mighty like
a bridegroom, the bull; who storms the light, who strikes
the loin with pleasure, fertile, sudden, and whole.
The bull a wind of capes, who shoulders
pike and horse, who takes the thrust with blood,
and glories in the gay darts, hooded,
a mane. He wavers for the barehead killer's
cloth, exulting; desperate; then still.

Then still and face to face, he knows
all this was lies: the boxer on his toes
weaved and feinted to deceive, the tart
Veronica was seductive and smart.
He who had been splendid and uncouth
stands warily for the sword-thrust now, the truth.

The people stands; and the soldier with the red cloth
still masks the gun, still flutters the pride
of the fighter. Yes, the sportsman may take sides
yet, hunter make a book.
But the bull knows he looks
at death. When the shade
lengthened the ring, he was betrayed.

O proud and stubborn still for the unfurled
sword, he who had been a world's
glory lowers the head that has hurled
kings high, to follow a bunting. Now the nape
is bare. The headsman rapes
it to the abrupt hilt.
Again in Spain blood spills.

Shadow and blood darken, now
towered Toledo lies below
the winy river flowing slow
westward, the Tagus-sky glows low.
Bishop and dowager bend the knee
to the crossed hilt, and the dogs are free.
The Moorish killers fold their cloaks
of light about them; like hawks
on wrists, sated, sit the picadors
horse-high, or in the laps of whores.
The racketeers roar.

I write a people's elegy
in sand, where blood stales. They
who died were simple, alone, never free.
Dusk covers them like blindness. I see
the killers meet the night in twos and threes.

In Memory of Ramon Lull

Miramar like a rocket climbs
the air. Below, the sea
draws feathers over nets, a cat's
cradle for the gunboats.
The scene is silent as a mime.

Not I, recalling seven, but Lull
seven hundred years ago
made this memorable; nor
idly eyeing the loved shore,
but in the vision of the full

man looked to do good greatly.
Here he built a school,
printed laborious Latin; taught
others the calm his vivid thought
nightly denied him, passionately.

And barefoot walked through Africa,
and planned a commonwealth
with Plato; reasoned, wrote songs.
Martyred under Moorish stones,
he did not hear the Cardinals' veto.

Who now remembers that ignorant
fanatic who prized
knowledge more highly than armour?
The sentry calls from Miramar
the dirge the Moorish mob once chanted,

and in the harbour, sea-planes are
heirs to the Italian
Cardinals. They have left nothing
of Lull but the words of gunmen
schooling soldiers, a hungry power.

Nothing? The delicate watercourses
Moors etched on Miramar
deny it. And he whom these
shamed with sudden tenderness,
Lull smiles from the blood-red roses.

And cries the dervish outlaw
yet, and the Papal Caesar.
Nor lacks examples of the faith
which made a victory of the death
of his Italian pupil Bruno,

who arrogantly gave the lie
to Popes; and, though he burned,
is resurrected every age.
Here in his island too the sage
shall live, the soldier die;

Miramar like a rocket light
its signal truth; and Bruno write
"Amen" to that page, Lull claimed
God and reason are the same.

THE DEATH OF W. B. YEATS

Maybe an elegy for that
fanatic Irishman comes pat,
seeing that he never knew
his native language, from a Jew:

seeing that he hawked his bones
among English, exile towns,
and sold the chronicles of his dead
for poetic gingerbread,

it is fitting I recall
another people used to sell
centuries of pride and hurt
for the precision of a word.

O yes, I also know the tears
strangling his Irish verse
because the handsome, alien lords
ride to hounds, and have their sport

with lovelier women than are bedded
under crofter quilts, or ghetto's.
Knowing why his passion dwelled
on Swift, I am not cynical.

For not to belittle, but to praise
Yeats, do I labour this;
and read his mind to understand
the eagles there, the power beyond

jealousy and bitterness
and the fantasies of wish.
All his angry dreams do not
hide the greatness of his thought.

I too take pride because a race
few are proud of, stamped my face.
I do not count its heroes, nor
what it suffered and forbore.

But eager, bitter, covetous too,
I look from Irishman to Jew:
Yeats is my example that
all that hunger can make great,

that generations hold my pen
to write the nobleness of men.
Their eagles in my eyes rehearse
his raging and triumphal verse.

The Heroic Moment

Keep up your bright bayonets, Moors; ere the acid
red dew unedges them. Blood like evening
eats the fine lines, the profile of the Cid;
and the heroic moment, Quixote is failing.

Sancho astraddle on his donkey enters
Madrid. The braying trumpeter commands
his island idiots with the word Romance.
The brazen hooves stamp in the arid land.

Was it romantic, Moors, at Badajoz:
Malaga betrayed, Guernica, the starved Asturias?
Not you wear glory like a wound, but those
on flowering stumps who fled from Figueras

to the French dunes, baffled, overwhelmed,
but uncowed. The Cid fled thus, thus lay Cervantes
in Moorish camps; yet made the broken helmet
a symbol for the matador and dancer.

All, all under the hooves of the ass. The song
the olive-pickers had from Lull is blown
out; and the doctor's skill, shared once among
dockers, learned from shepherds, is overthrown.

All pride of workmanship in Europe dies.
The Spanish soldier with the iron foot
sings bawdy to the walls of peace, and hears
the echo break the olive in the root.

Hears the Carpathians answer, Corsica,
the Irish Sound. Now comes night with the Moor
from China to the Southern Cross, baring
the jewelled hilt, the bomber's silver, where

the ore, precious as stones, aches to be forged.
There is an end of those who used the day.
The earth goes underground. Hooves in the dark
beat iron. And the trumpet thunder brays.

I for a generation whom the lathe
gave living and pleasure, who ploughed, thought freely,
speak this its epilogue. We did not save
the gift of man from animal fury,
failing to meet the gunmen with the gun
sooner: but, sullen, thought that too, defeat.
And that Cervantes's heritage was but man,
so he died for, but men to treat

with the beast's hoof, the odds of the dark. Yet we are not lost
at last, though over our graves the Moors
pile pyramids for a world in arms. Yes, the beast's
stamp shall yet make dust of the beast, the boor
be shamed by boors; and the romantic lust
become a horror to its blinded poor.

This is my prophecy: destruction runs on
destruction; but the hero, though he lies
dead, lives. Underground he is humming
pride at the bench, the peasant's sureness.
The bayonets blunt with blood, Moors: you shall yet sing
the resurrection of the Cid with us.

THE GREAT

Chartres, the Degas bronzes, cast
a gleam on France. In Ireland, Yeats
or exiled Spenser, Dryden in England -
these made their generations great.

Thus Dante, or Goethe at Weimar, once
struck a match, and drenched the lout
with light, and shamed the fool. But all
that ends. The lands which blazed, burn out.

No longer are the strong content
to be praised as was Pericles,
alive in his people. Now the mouth
must be a bugle for the brutal.

Wessel the singing pimp, D'Annunzio
a paid agent, the tall maddened

builders of fortresses - they give
this generation of addicts

the illusion of power, the real
war in whimpers. Did Cervantes say
"Peace"? But not to Spain. Was Greece
Plato's Republic? Yesterday.

The small have conquered; westward stamp
their level hooves. The drugged, the jealous,
or crazed with longing, overwhelm
the cities where the great were fellows.

The light of France, like music, sinks
under the Channel wave; all proud
speech, Sidney's, Cobbett's, drowns.
The dark blinds Milton; and the loud

rumour tears down tune, tears buildings
and men to paper tattered. Death
lies heavily on the great in silence:
ruins of masonry and breath.

SOME HAPPY HOURS

Some happy hours, perhaps, are still
unspent. The wounded tissues hoard them
in spite of the destructive will.
And still the eyes bite through the mordant

for green, for hope: to see the days
delicately walk down avenues
of sureness, and with shadow blaze
the shadows whence the light renews.

Tunnels the wish drives, that the parched
muscle its metal quench, the lens
become an eye again. Their arches
from every organ of the sense

spring, shuttle, like the mole, below
the mountain present, this sick head.
Are these the brain's despairing burrow
in doomed lands, to the certain dead?

Or is it they who pith the mountain
with indecision like a worm?

sink shafts the dynamiters storm?
Or will they tap the light in fountains?

O velvet senses in a caul,
always unmet and always feared:
it was not bravery to fall
rather than that you should be heard.

I am that coward of the will,
denied your touch. Let me be strong
to pit the slaggy, present wrong
once, with the body's unlearned skill;

to let the future grow deliberate,
deep, as a foetus, from the prick
and taste. There is a heart to tick,
a mind to mean, which never let

the tumour of the will, a feared
folly of words, bow them. Uncowed
they call the tissues, spend your hoard;
call the man, be proud.

THE DEATH OF ERNST TOLLER

1
Time stops. The ticking pulse stops. But
the pendulum of the hanged men
beats on. His clockwork feet still drum
the door to stillness that was shut.

Not with the patter of the breasting
runner, breathless; but inexorable
as a blind man tapping for pennies,
he stumbled through his everlasting

dark, here; wandered the cold
charity; and leaped at last
clean through the wheel misfortune, the
machine of the heart, to this still threshold.

2
He is dead, not because loneliness
and exile limped with him for years;
but that greatness a life long
had beckoned him, been gracious, close,

been all but grasped: yet out of reach --
he with a sudden gesture smashed
the muscle with the memory
in the one, convulsive twitch.

Because he knew the gross forgetting
shabbying his name, he tore it up:
instant to meet disaster, rather
than the collapse of whispering;

instant to hurry into shame,
because convinced that shame awaited
him, and a world; because he read
the ruin of an age in his name.

He is among those tall defeated
to whom the heartbreak grace was fatal,
all suffering a despair,
who were a mind without a sheath:

pointed with vanishing hands to goodness,
and, when a civilisation failed,
struck once and violently the clock
thirteen, a silly season news.

3
Let the whisperers leave the door,
that his congested ear shall hear
no more the roaring of defeat
in the overwhelmed dark, no more

fear, no more pain, no pity.
Let the brave lift him from the latch,
and for a moment by the great
let him be carried shoulder-high.

To the Fallen

Though the event yet waits, I write
this verse for those whom, when it chooses,
war pins fantastic to the side
of glory like a paper posy,

the fallen. Honour them, because
they were a mannish honour's whim in
the play with death at pitch and toss
for penny stakes: the fallen women.

Not, in the casual mesh of mine
and trigger blasted, men: but these
trapped by deliberate design
of men on man - they are the heroes.

Them strident, them indifferent, missing
the shape of tragedy, yet great,
prophecy like an ember kissed
with peace, before a war betrayed

and made them outposts of disaster
a generation plans for man.
Honour their falling, who have mastered
the accident of hurt, the chance

machine; but face to face have seen
men taking pleasure in the wish
destruction, and the thinking mind
glory that animals are unleashed.

THE IMPERSONAL TRAGEDY

The impersonal tragedy sweeps on. From Spain
to China, thence to the troubled Baltic, swings
Oedipus in the circle of his pain.
The cities sicken with the plague foreboding.

I among men, the makers of islands, shore
the walls of the heart with blindness; find two trees
to make a country seat, retreat; and snore
nightly the fevered, fervent wish for peace.

The hope of happiness leaps like a pulse,
secret and shameful, under our anguished lives.
Indifference cheats, then drowns; snatching in handfuls
meals and rumours, the comfort of wives,

water. It is not this way comes salvation,
yet knows no other way. And if the strong
master a different future, their notion
swamps common ill with individual wrong.

I do not plead the fancy of a summer,
a respite from fear while the sun shines, trusting
to luck and shutting the mind to what's coming;
neither the glib defeatism of the nasty;

nor bitter hopelessness of those exhausted
by years against odds, who nurse themselves with dreams
the universal terror may at last
smash all authority, and make a freedom.

Mine is the pleading of those common men
who in the shadow of destruction shudder,
but seek the sun, are pitifully content
with private happiness, to share with others

bed and board, to do their work by rote;
yet value what's done well. Do not think ill
of their designs because they never thought
to murder wrong, and be their own freewill.

Because the event has grown too great to yield
to bands like theirs, the event is not the greater.
They are not weak because their hope is killed.
Failing now, they will be masters later.

Let them lie easy between breasts some nights
still yet: there is nothing desperate they can do.
Yet trust that when you are urgent, they will fight
for whet is great, greatly; and that the true

will conquer and be honest, though they slept
helpless for years. They are the undefeated,
whom generations have believed inept,
but never will, for never have, retreated.

ALEXANDER'S DRUM

Some savage whom the Greeks called god,
miracle-mongering in Asia,
still lords it in history: still fights
the Truck Act and the Bill of Rights.

What has the imagination seized
to make the story of his brutal
dominion an epitome
of power for every century;

buckling the dates of ministers
and glib encyclicals beneath
his emblem like a brooch? They fall
in folds of fact from him, the symbol:

falls Carthage, falls the march on Rome,
the rape of Austria, Marathon,
all on that Alexander's drum.
And the recording angel thumbs

Hansard or *News from Nowhere*, weeping
still to find terror everyday,
and hear The Army Councils briskly
damning the conscript with the risk.

Because some schoolman quack was pleased
to linger on a heathen fable,
a thousand years of history
are lavish with the stain of glory:

Poor Law and Unemployed Insurance
are not a match for oratory
a gunman hires to ensure
profits for another year,

snug beneath the bright hysteria
of Jingo and the wrongs of Troy.
Because a world was taught to honour
Sidney and Greece, again the banners

break out, the poor go hungry, grief
circles with ravens overhead.
The House of Commons waits to hear
Europe explode at Jenkins' ear.

THE WORD

What the word did, the word undoes. It said
"In the beginning", and shall count the dead.

It gave the ape a man; the man, a God.
The restless prophet with the word was shod.

It built a tower. It made a law. It blessed
the city walls, and called the stranger guest.

Greece was a miracle because the word
crowded its mouth with paradox and surd.

Jostled the courts of Italy with light,
and gave the poet words, the painter sight.

The word it was which touched the faggot Spain.
The will to know sprang from the word in pain.

This drove Linnaeus. This made Berkeley heard.
The breath of science was the hungry word.

It taught the poor a right; the right a need;
the need, rebellion. And the word was deed.

Was strong, was supple; overcame; was fond,
in generations when the word was bond.

The generations end. The right retreats.
The word of honour is a word for cheats.

They wronged the word: and now the word has read
their deed in writing, and has spelled it, dead.

The bankrupt people cries to words, and breaks.
The word has made it, and word unmakes.

Our Age Is Beginning

The gaslight poet, Ichabod,
mourns the departed glory of God:
Christ on the Mount and Noah's Ark -
his paper islands in the dark.
Like amber glows the past in rhyme:
a broken column, lilac time,
snatches of Dante and Purcell;
Antigone with asphodel -
a halo of nostalgic tears
on waterwings and chandeliers.
All these were culture; he compares
them with the present, and despairs
that history no longer screens
the market-gardens and machines.

Leave him, the pursuer of self in mirrors.
What he denounces, yes, are errors.
History has always made them, crass
as schoolboy howlers; for history has
no inky fingers, it must be taken
red-handed, overcome, forsaken
and re-made. History is gas

and daylight saving, *Hudibras,*
justice and greyhounds; the abyss
of suicide. History is.

Is sure; yet something common to
all these; which underneath them grew
like bone to give them shape, or rippled
from universal joint to nipple.
Some skill on which the engineer
lingers: the reading of verniers
by navvies, the draughtsman's pencil in
the rough hand, the driver in his cabin.
Yes, the common man has fingers so fine
that all the world is his design.
Other ages ended when a king
changed his fancy: but ours is beginning -
beginning in the hands of boys, alive
in the craftsman and the diver,
beginning, beginning. At the building-plot and
the gear-cutter, on the allotment
it grows, it fountains: finer than Venice,
the precision of mechanics.

War and Peace

Peace, he smokes a big cigar;
picks your pocket - or was it war?

Ask the trader looting China,
Which hires you? How should I know?

Peace is blander, war kills faster:
two names, but a single master.

Toss your penny to the rich:
heads for war, and tails for - which?

Tinker, tailor, poor man, toss;
the rich man with the pearl won't lose.

He nods; the spinning penny stops.
The poor man in the trenches drops.

War, he smokes his bomb at Nice;
picks your pocket - or was it peace?

THE BIGOT

Maybe the bigot's me; and those
I mock for birds-of-parasite,
love a freedom I've forgone
because I think the poor are wronged:
because I know the poor are right.

Maybe. Maybe when Dryden shelved
*Mac Fleckn*oe and the gift of scorn,
he'd learnt a tolerance that paid
cash and, yes, credit; and was made
a better man because he fawned.

Wordsworth among his stamps, or these
whom holy water desiccates,
Auden and Eliot: maybe I
wrong their humility when I say
it falls to furtiveness and hate.

I see them in the holy places
shuffle with masochists to mass;
and the denial of the wise
lowers like a shame their eyes,
in whom my eyes once read greatness,

maybe, because I'm astigmatic.
Yes, that a boy in Spain could want
when lice might wanton, is less moving
to those whose eyes have known the love
of God in buggery and cant.

Yet, while that boy to man and brute
grows, by no urge but poverty's,
the ruined choristers shall raise
their liquid lips for none I praise;
but for the punishment of disease.

Nor shall I think the Pope a man
till he, who exiled usury,
lets that anger be re-born
in loathing of the Roman loan
he lives on fatly in his city;

and sheathes the black encyclicals
against the striker in a rag,
and before God with banners strides

among the banner-bearing, laggard,
at Hyde Park on Sunday night.

Eliot or Auden: until then
I mock your chivalrous talk of times
when poverty shall be no crime.
but understanding cure the itch
of randy, lock-outs, and the rich;

and lift my head no higher
than a soldier's tourniquet, the hiss
of gas a miner feels, to stand,
the wounds of God red in my hands -
Auden and Eliot, look at this!

If thus, a headstrong man, I wrong you,
I still am right to be mistaken,
and passionately to assert
we are betrayed when we are hurt,
we are the less for your forsaking:

to speak my heresy of contempt for
your brokers' order, that invents
riches from chaos, and a God
to underwrite the risk of wealth.
I am the heretic of truth

for whom your justice, privilege,
stinks from the feet of bishops through
the hogskin and the holy wine.
Blake is my example, shining
because the sweepers climbed his brow.

O, Blake too fell, and Browning who
had once despised his treacherous leader;
falling, they pitched headlong, not
whimpering, into whatever fever
ran with their ending life to riot.

Yes, I like them may fail; like Kraus
who'd traced a war's distraught infection
gangrene the world: yet died a fool.
Like him, I here disown that evil
years ere it may distort the bone.

Therefore I write my name, to say,
if ever I grow hypocrite,
you shall remember, men in pits,

that I throw down that possible sham;
being proud of nothing but what I am --

am one with you, and shall remain so,
but for some tic of age, some halving
of spirit, not mine. This self
reaches your self and is its greetings:
that man and poet are a meeting.

A Day at the Races

The tic-tac man had been a poet;
the jockey saved to own a pub.
The past was beer, the future pickles
to these who gambled for their grub.

The bookie slapped his bag and shouted
the odds that either should survive
in markets where the iron shares
hardened a point to one point five.

Only the horses danced their stirrups,
pure Degas, in a green of grace:
ignorant of Swift, not bred to wonder;
content a horse should stay the race.

Prologue

For a Living Newspaper on 'Oil'

1
Lawrence, the solemn playboy, proved it all:
that camels gallop, Arabs die for plunder.
The dynamite blew fountains in the sand,
and every duchess clapped her hands with wonder.

O yes, he made romance come true: rebellion
at twenty pounds a head -- the Ruby M. Ayres
sheikh performed what the drab had imagined,
and paid himself no rake-off but despair.

What was it drove him through those desert spaces
to run to sand in motor-boats and lorries?
The ache for self; the greed of power; the dream
that glamour shines from kings and condottieri.

This the rich sold to kitchen-maids and dons,
an Arab empire or a Jewish soil;
then found a hero to invest illusion,
to pitch their frontiers where the pipe-line runs,
and, in the holy places, strike for oil.

EPILOGUE

For a Living Newspaper on 'Oil'

2
The flowering oil, the fountain-sweet explosion
is a heart-beat under rocks and runs in sand.
The feet of martyrs, burning, were anointed,
tracing its pipe-lines through the holy land.

Not milk and honey dropped so rich an ooze
at supper, when the chosen people rested,
as brims the salad-bowl the board-room circles,
Anglo-Iranian profits re-invested.

Probed for with drills or roaring from the gushers,
the unguent blessing stutters at the wheel,
hammers on pistons, is the strength of cities
-- see the *Financial Times*, and mark down steel.

Because its blood is what the desert squanders,
the scrub is thirsty for the blood we lavish;
watching with jackals from the lost oases,
until the night shall crunch the bones of soldiers,
the drilling-rigs, the rusted engines ravished.

THE THUMB IN THE MARGIN

Thirty years a fool, and two a boor
put me to school, and taught me to despise
tipster and bigot, and the man of rule,
whoever claims to live by being wise;
and that no nostrum but contempt will cure
two years a boor, and thirty years a fool.

I gave myself this year to make amends
for all that idle discontent, which flattered
I must be tragic, or make history. -
History rolls its own thunder latterly,

playful as a puppy; and, as animal, rends
the paper promise with a clap of glory.

No longer is disaster what is dreamed
between the lids of what I feared, and dare.
It is the eyeball of the world which wakes
on roofs of nightmare, where the moonlight chalks
her icy orbit, under a sky at war;
and sees the craters swinging nearer, screaming.

How should his story dare to make a man
match that defeat, because he lived in want
of happiness, like others; but learned to choose
to sleep alone and think the nights well spent;
loving a girl like reason, and being then
most moved when all her reasons mastered his?

Yet let me tell the story, for a fable
either of spirit, or the famished passion
which bites the apple world and spits the core.
I shared my folly with any man of fashion,
finding it no less for being reasonable,
nor, because it is pitiful, think his the more.

A Polish Jew spent his precocious childhood
on the Sudeten border; and had it plain
that such a one could never live at home,
live he the year long with a love in Spain -
that, too, sleeps in the amber of my blood.
This year I wait in England for the bombs.

Two revolutions bitterly slaked the guns,
with bitter men, of Germany – there came
the starveling boy to find an English slum
sanctuary, or a knife to scratch my name
on school and college; while the revolutions,
silently, were betrayed; I heard no drums.

What might that hungry mind, that hungry mouth
have heard, had not my ear been satisfied
with abstract spaces for geometry,
abstruse music of a verse which lied.
They gave assurance to content a youth
to take a mistress, and write poetry.

Even under the drums is a pulse: love
can be momentous, and the blood suddenly
feel in the spinning head the centrifuge

pull on the middle of the heart; nor be
uneasy that the piling force may move
into destruction when the beat grows huge.

The eye will see a girl, and etch the error,
acid, upon ambition; and be devout
the act of seeing had been made for this,
the act of thinking is her thought read out;
and that her mind can be the burning mirror
wherein my life and hers shall hiss and fuse.

I, yes, saw such a one; and served my time,
a Jacob, chastely, to possess that riches;
grudging no more the labour than to share
what all must envy, because each bewitches.
Hers was the breathless ladder I learned to climb
where sweet and stinging went the singing air.

I hold to-night that night I took her hand
so great a happiness, the last of nights
but equalled it; nor would forgo for either
two years of pain I wrestled for her sight -
so great a pain, I cannot understand
she charmed and loved me, and was true in neither.

And count those too, how should I forget, the years
we smuggled happiness; were constant; drove
two hundred miles to spend a night in love.
We did not sense the sultry Europe when
we pressed for mastery, and left in tears:
drive back two hundred miles, but drive alone.

Neither do I belittle the pain I cost her
because, being headstrong and intolerant
and wretched with the loss of days undone
watching out nights, I would be dominant;
cruel when angry, and when glad, preposterous;
and, being lonely, made her be alone.

I, who foretold all tragedies: the wounds
of Austria, Spain crucified, the walls
ghostly with soldiers on the wine-bled Rhine -
1 knew them all, but ours, original,
because the mounting reason is caught in bounds
by men whose passion masks the fury of swine.

The tears of angels are the sweat of torture;
light seeping through the page flows from their stain,

and history's, the thumb in the margin, leaving
the angel print because these flow again:
because a man wants certainty of future,
a girl would rather love than live by grieving.

Would rather be a woman than created
in any high imaginary room
a ghost on water where the light is clear
to hear my words re-echo like a doom
hers, because I thought we two were mated;
would sooner be another's than my dear.

Dear, be forgiving, for I wronged, and wrong you;
yet let me speak, I thought that all would fail,
world and friends, peace, the dignity of men;
but not we two. The merciless thought like hail
drives me to-night because I have seen you, true,
forswear the true, and let the best be beaten.

It is not arrogance which makes me cry
there are no men like me, who hold the good
higher than every personal whim or hurt;
contemptuous and despairing, yes, but
for whom worlds bear, that they may live. They die.
You stamped that man deliberately in dirt.

You made a rant of what had been heroic.
I had thought such men as I should hold to, still,
the desert tragedies of Greece and Spain.
All, all is nothing now but obstinate will.
The strong philosopher creeps to the stoic;
the tragic hero makes a show of pain.

Cries, world, be burst with medlar ripeness; fall,
you ashes that ferment the sweating apple.
The willow stump shall glow at night, the light
by day run rivers in the fallow, dappled.
You made a mockery of the man, to call
destruction, who had once believed in right.

Do not take trouble even to smile: I beckon
none to destroy but me; none to destruction
but that proud man was me. The time is ready
the man of folly be a man of action,
the two year boor forget the bitter reckoning
and walk the street which rinses as it bleeds.

My English Miss, my snob that stints and stings,
I shall not love the like of you again.
The face I fumble shall say tenderness
to bread or hawker, being easy, open,
company for men and at home with things;
the mind be simple but be sharp as these,

who come to knowledge not by will but use,
live with themselves and husband no regrets.
Teach me to speak like her, homely and searching,
to men in trams or buying cigarettes;
what people think of when they hear the news,
which councillors are dead, what soldiers marching.

Their life is cancered with the rich, the hard
and iron-faced; the iron masters; all
who buy the poor for lunch and spend the title
on afternoons with fear and cagoulards –
the powerful, the possessed. And Europe falls
to all their evil because we abide it.

I with my cynical illusions: you,
mercenary of your comfort, with the foible
only the lesions of professional women
were left to cure: we are responsible.
I was deceived; but you remain the tool
and symbol of the age of simony.

To-day I set myself the resurrection
of hands which died in silence; and will re-make
this little gift of bitterness, to score
blood from the humble on the day which walks
the slums the great have never found before;
and, though a stranger at the door of action,

and thirty years a fool and two a boor,
submit to courage as if to ridicule,
content to be a need to these I need;
fail in myself, but must in them succeed
who never made a gesture to prefer
the two year boor, or thirty years a fool.

1939–1973 (Christmas Card Poems)

1939

Now good King Carol turns his ass
with Holofernes through the Khyber Pass;
all the wise men of the East bring gems
to the pipe-line tap at Bethlehem.
And the child, adored, may keep
all gifts but the gift of sleep;
all but peace; and never see
the shadow cast below the tree.
While the kings with gun and drum
ride towards Jerusalem
to the outstretched, blessed palms
of Christ the child, to present arms.

1939 (B)

IT was no star the Magi heard
but the stutter of a bird,
that in falling struck a spark
from the milling vanes of dark.
They did not guess what engines would
spatter all his breast with blood,
nor how shameful we should think
the white feathers of his wing.
Yet that ghost or bird shall climb
iron sky and hooded time

S. Rennie (ed.), *Jacob Bronowski: Selected Poems,*
https://doi.org/10.1007/978-3-032-19597-5_5

till the drumming engines spill:
every bird but this be still.

1940

Jupiter and Saturn played.
The age was broken and re-made.
A rocket rose from Bethlehem.
Christ marched with the Orangemen;
till, diving, the exploding light
struck to-day, and charred it white.

The rocket roars and plunges out.
Saturn and Jupiter turn about.
No child again shall put to shame
the gunsights trained on Bethlehem;
while ice-cap, omen, march to birth
the orbit of the screaming earth.

1947

THE voice of God that spoke and struck
Was the cuckoo in the clock.
The exiles in the garden heard
The engine tremble in the bird,
Sobbing throat and iron bill:
Time on his springy wheel stood still.

Time began and time runs down.
The voices in the garden drown.
No God from his machine unhands
The exile with a mouth of sand.
The clockwork cuckoo on the hill,
Abrupt and wheeling, stoops to kill.

1947 (B)

BETWEEN the olive and the sloe
The summer comet hissed in snow.
An instant his chaotic plume
Scrawled the sullen air with doom,

Then like a legend headlong fell.
The ice rang iron like a bell.

Yet that semaphore of death
Signalled a birth from Nazareth;
And, seeding, the exploding shower
Conceived a childhood and a flower.
Grave from that ancient waste there grow
The crowns of olive and of sloe.

1948

Beyond the manger shines the tree,
Beyond the angel, Galilee.
The symbols keep their ancient rows,
Nothing withers, nothing grows;
And jubilant or tragic birth
Are bench-marks on the frozen earth.

Yet the star is charged with power:
The nucleus will explode or flower.
The angel with the swept-back wings
Contains a life that screams or sings.
And not a saviour but a child
Bursts from the symbol and runs wild.

1949

Everything was snow and gold.
The lantern glistered on the cold.
The magi from their jewelled wrists
Shook a brightness as they blessed.
Only the centre, grave and mild,
Held, secret but unreconciled,
The dark head of the new-born child.

Everything had been foretold.
The comet flashed, the planets rolled.
The pilgrims, where they worshipped, found
The snow swept and the clockwork wound.
Only the future slept and smiled,
Wilful, innocent, and wild
With mischief as a new-born child.

1951

No apparition drowned the air
With music. Everything was bare
And usual. No one cried "Beware",

Because a scrawl of snow betrayed
The childish hand, and overlaid
Its lifeline with a cross, the jade

And gold with crystal. Gravely, calm,
The snowflake in the infant palm
Lay like a star, a thorn, a wound, or balm.

1952

The snoring man, the peevish moke
Woke in the dark barn. Neither spoke.
A sense of being still pursued
Made everything around them crude
As nightmare. Grey lay on stone and bone.
They heard the girl in labour moan.

Her groan struck like a match, that scratched
An instant dazzle in the thatch.
Pain like a fuse or vapour trail
Climbed the comet by the tail.
When the child wailed, they knew the night
Had set posterity alight.

1953

Under the raging equinox
Mary conceived. The weathercocks
Crowed and tumbled into June.
She watched them tread the harvest moon,
Sleepless all summer. In October
The weeping virgin died, a sober
Child took her face and, wearing there
An innocence beyond despair,
Put away the months of grief.
Snow sifted on the gale-torn leaf.
Warm in the winter sunshine smiled
The child upon her newborn child.

1954

A landscape where the scrub disdains
The mountain. Hunger licks the plains.
Across the frontier, barbed, the spivs
Jostle among the fugitives -

How could the hunted girl resist
(Blood in her eyes, and amethyst)
The child's impatience to be born?
She saw too late his hands were torn.

Happy, passionate, and come
Headlong from his mother's womb,
He thought the glowing barn was home,

And never guessed its friendly smells
Were breathed only by animals.
Men waited for him with long nails.

1955

An ice age and a rage of heat
Taught the prodigious sun deceit.
The prophets thundered at eclipse
Oracular in racing tips.

Till Isaac Newton showed the Pope
The clockwork in the horoscope
And, because each hated each,
Split the spectrum like a peach.

Now the savage blazing tree
Must relight the century,
Doubt and passion form a boy
To spin the sunbeam like a toy -
A cat's cradle of light that hums
Gold from golden thumb to thumb.

1956

The desert is a rose, and glows.
The thorn that burned for Moses blows
Blood-red among the mortar-bursts;
The desert is a rose that thirsts.

The desert is a rose, and fades:
Here humanity was made.
Here my forebears from the sand
Scratched with bare hands a holy land.

They through dark millenia kept
Their longing for the land that slept;
Until their children rose to sow
The seed from which all roses grow.

Now the raiders walk the hill,
Tank and tank-trap meet to kill.
Behind the dunes the dervish waits-
The desert is a rose, and hates.

The desert is a rose that weeps:
Where Moses struck the rock, there seeps
An oil-slick, a mirage with weeds.
The desert is a rose, and bleeds.

1957

Snow should have fallen upward to eclipse
The moon, and virgin forests should have burned,
The strata should have cracked their metal lips.

But nothing spoke. The earth slept where it lay.
Only among the planets as they turned
A comet signalled that the night was day.

In sixteen centuries Copernicus
(Until the supernova split the sky)
Died unregarded with his master-key.

The omens for an age of miracles
Lope on their orbits overhead, and we
Ask them to tell us what they prophesy.
We gape at wonders and forget to see.

1958

Faster than light and cold as absolute,
The edge of darkness races in pursuit
Of this expanding leaf, this Christmas tree
Of veins in which I hold the galaxy.

It is my hand, from which there streams and rips
The cosmic shift, red to the fingertips,
And what the flying shadow hunts is me.

Some astral bang, some primum mobile
Rocketed both of us, the headlong Bear
And me, into the incandescent air.
The motion that we share entails it all:
The virgin birth, the carol tune, the tall
Luminous star that prophesies - although
Its only secret is that children grow.

Faster than night and cold as Helium II,
The edge of shadow races to undo
The secret of creation, the abrupt
Choice of a womb or atom to erupt,
And what the flying darkness hunts is you.

1960

I, having built a house, reject
The feud of eye and intellect,
And find in my experience proof
One pleasure runs from root to roof,
One thrust along a streamline arches
The sudden star, the budding larches.

The force that makes the winter grow
Its feathered hexagons of snow,
And drives the bee to match at home
Their calculated honeycomb,
Is abacus and rose combined.
An icy sweetness fills my mind,

A sense that under thing and wing
Lies, taut yet living, coiled, the spring.

1961

It was a star, it was a bird,
It was a toy, it was absurd -
A cataract of rumour roared
And tumbled when the omen soared,
Till John the judge and Tom the thief
Paddled their feet in unbelief.

What was there to believe? A boy
Rose like a bird, fell like a toy.
All the wisdom in his head
Made the lad a little mad.
Yet, falling or in flight, he had
The splendour of the renegade,

The kiss that from a god unlocks
The man, the touch that bursts the rock.
He, a prodigy of speech,
Made the law a laughing-stock,
That a common doubt might teach
Tom the thief and John the judge
To bury their dividing grudge.

1962

There must have been a time when fate
Was clear and unelaborate;
When gods pursued their loves, and kings
Murdered in silk; and underlings
Led silent, parish lives, for fear
Pride would be beautiful and dear.

All was sabotaged the night
Mary the rebel took to flight,
And rocked the poles, and overturned
The tables whereon incense burned.
The child she carried, when he woke,
Spoke to the ox and broke his yoke.

That was two millennia past.
Still in the gaming-rooms the last
Golden, exiled kings enjoy
The miracles they grudged the boy.
Still the gods fall and still survive.
Yet when the parish shouts with pride
It is the boy they crucified
Who smiles, and speaks, and is alive.

1963

Aquinas argued how an arrow flies,
And I, snug in a jet, nod and look wise.
What rusty habit satisfies my mind

With metaphors my childhood left behind,
Or makes me feel our age is understood
In the vernacular of Robin Hood -
Simply because, seven centuries ago,
Aquinas set his cross-bow in the snow?
We all are crucified by what we know.

Along the avenues of yew and stone
The slip-stream whistles through a megaphone,
Topples the ancient images, and shouts
To be acknowledged by the lay-abouts.
The drifts of history, the ice of dearth
Melt like an armour from the flying earth.
Another logic struggles into birth.

1964

Blue as a dream and fabulous,
Suspended between time and space,
Here hangs, immaculate in glass,
The tropic bubble of the year that's past.

I tip the glass, and suddenly
See the snow in flurries fly:
A trick of weather in a toy
Shakes my memory with joy.
So winter used to bite, and storm
Raked me long ago and froze me warm.

1965

This is the coast the lemmings reached;
They did not drown but simply beached.
Here after agonies (and less)
They found the go-go star Success,
The goddess in the wilderness,
Who shook her breast and blessed the west.

She beckons from the burning-glass,
Medusa with a face of brass,
And lucid as magnesium strip
Writes with her sunset fingertip
A rain-check to the Hall of Fame:
Make a cross and put your name.

1966

One of the magi brought, to match
The lapis lazuli, a flint:
Folded like a child, the print
Of man slept in the artifact.

So in the caves of India bloom
The convoluted hands of gods
Waiting till the millennium nods
To burst the blueprint from the womb.

The lights along the Ganges run
From Christmas to the fingertips,
And monuments and weather-ships
Articulate the same design

That prophetic man began
When from the stone he chipped the plan.

1967

He wore sandals and a beard;
What he said had not been cleared.
A Socratic innocence
Made it sound like common sense -
Peace for me, good will to you -
It was so old, it wasn't true.

Drugged as he was with parable,
Mutinous, boyish, down at heel,
His captors saw they had it made:
A gypsy leading a crusade
Of children. Lightly, when he gave
Them flowers, they threw them in his grave.

1968

Beyond the walls of dogma bloom
(You must believe me) fields of broom.
The birds shout and the beeches shiver
Light in the sky under the river.
And clouds of lilac sigh to reach
Lovers laughing as they touch.

Our blessings on the heads of state
Who lead us, o not there, but straight -

Who weigh the gravity of laws
(Pot against a bombing pause)
Measure the parallels, assess
Whether Prague is worth a mass,
And in the dusk of overkill
Pontificate about a pill.

While still the walls of dogma nose
Towards the stations of the cross.

1969

Clap your hands and reach your toes,
This is how the infant grows,
Joining the known to what he tries.
The world is what is touched from thigh to sky.

Walking was bound to teach him soon
Footloose to scuff the magic moon,
And circumnavigate with glee
The deserts with the names of seas.
The universe is there to prove,
To range and change, to understand and move.

So on a Sunday, after grace,
He poked a peep-hole into space,
To watch beyond Tranquility
The planets light their Christmas tree.
That was when he saw they lied;
They were cinders, and those worlds had died.

The distant summer afternoon
Stirred in the dustbowl of the moon.
It touched him as he turned in flight.
From continents once faint with night
He heard the future call him: Come,
Bring your courage, head for home,
Be proud, be loud,
            and love the earth,
                    it lives, it gives.

1970

Again the desert re-deploys
Its haunted armies of despair,
And conjures from the trembling air
The ancient madness, to destroy.
We wait upon the imminent
Massacre of the innocents.

On such a night, a frightened fate
Tipped off the holy surrogate,
And luckily no patriot men
Hijacked the flight to Egypt then.
Yet when Joseph had that dream
He heard a thousand infants scream.

We celebrate a child's escape
From the carnage and the rape:
What became of all the rest?
Providence no doubt knew best.
Now we wait for providence
To save the other innocents.

1971

Always in flight, pell mell, farewell,
Spreadeagled between two hotels,
Breathless in Cuzco, grave in Greece,
In Altamira ill at ease,
I wake and in the darkness hear
The earth move under me in fear.

What have they done, the lidless faces
Made of stone in holy places,
The gargoyles on the roof at Rheims,
The Easter Island gods in teams,
Who, seeming to be raised to save,
Curse the living from the grave?

High on the tel of Jericho
I saw a - what? a boy below,
And every gesture, every bone,
Drew its menace from the stone.
Where in these deserts shall be born
The child without a crown of thorns?

1972

Genetics has a monkish rule
That virgin birth produces girls.
Maybe Jesus played it cool:
Laughed at the disarray of curls
And chromosomes, and with an arch
Submission to his destined part,
Said the household things that march
Through two millennia to the heart.

1973

With what contempt the Scots defined
The sly betrayal of their kind,
Blasting with prophetic rage
The desecration of the age.

Some electric Pharisee
Having bugged the Christmas tree
Or muzzled them with privilege
Gave their tongue an acid edge

To fix a synonym for rape
Without benefit of tape,
And assure posterity
No mincing prince will go scot-free.

CHAPTER 6

1939–1974 (Other Poems)

[The Images of Violence]

The images of violence possess me
like nightmare. Sleep comes to caress
the eyes with blood, slaver the fearful
mouth. All dreams are the dead in tears.

Whom the sea spared, war takes. The unborn are defeated
before conceived. The brave are hated.
Those who fled murder, take arms. Slumped rot
the young, or at attention in the humped
trenches. The old wander the snow till tramps
sell them. They die with broken mouths in camps.

Nightly thus befriended, I live with death
like lust. These wounds speak on my breath.
It is the dark age over Europe, like
a steel or glacier in the white night, strikes
dumb, strikes down with horror all my thought.
Therefore are the dead my succour: distraught,
but still unyielding: whom silence overwhelms,
but for whom deeds were real. Because the still
and iron future comes to make an end
of speech, my hand for help seeks these smashed hands.

Forgive me, violence, and silent reader,
this meeting face to face and the crowded
procession, the stiff bloody images. Soon

S. Rennie (ed.), *Jacob Bronowski: Selected Poems*,
https://doi.org/10.1007/978-3-032-19597-5_6

you shall be spared them; the burning will be noon.
The lout, the cruel, the fanatic shall be
heirs of my verse. They are for whom I see
the unspeakable visions, for whom suffer
the dead to share my bed and be brothers.
It is apt that terror and hate are my themes
ere the trooper burns this and the reader screams.
A generation faces the dark:
night must thicken my voice, and your stark
eyes read their last in blood.
After, all writing will be falsehood.

[HER BODY]

Her body and its slight, delightful face
sleep. Now the flesh forgoes
its mastery; and her dreams are those
the soldier cherished, though he loved her less,

who south through winter walked, to die
for her in Spain: but died for me. Nothing
he did so overwhelming
with loss is as her slack, contented thigh

nestling mine in sleep, without forgetting
his untouched. Soldier who fought
for what is good, to be free, to choose:
visit her eyes kindly, because
they must remember it was you they sought,
when they chose me to prove them free in choosing.

[NOW THE TURBULENT LIVES]

Now the turbulent lives end
in quinsy. The great grow crotchety.
Arid comes Spring the machine
leading the prodigy,

the young with vanes, with the eyes
of rifle-sights, facing the sun.
Two generations brunt: the old
whom their blood has undone,

but they lived; and to the young comes
their exact day. Alone the bred
in war, helpless, we whom war haunts,
were always dead,

and starveling, middle-aged, sit by
while boys draw plans to join the great
with thermite; and the generals
smile at their lying-in-state.

Yet we had blood, and were not grown
gouty; and knew the use
of prisms in humility,
and the sifting centrifuge --

yes, were the men who might have made
Utopia: knowing evil
and the heart's and the head's remedy;
but stood exhausted in the cavil

of young and old who run to death
for glory, for assurance. Never forgive
us, world we failed, which failed
to make us live,
that rich in passion
and with muscled minds, who might
have saved you, left you plunging
here, below the light.

[SLOWLY THE ABSCESS]

Slowly the abscess discontent, which seeps
in secret, tightens my gums. The poisoned blood
piles like a bore the raging temples, races
to limitless anger in the hands, and floods

the brain with bitterness I knew unworthy
three years ago. What was the needle stabbed
this puss into a body as generous
in bandying friendship as the mind was apt?

Age like a carbuncle, the flowering cancer
of idleness, and sickness like a wound,
these had their shares. But that which mastered them
was the betrayal of tremendous friends.

It is too late to speak them ill, whom years
I gave my substance, not stinting the rich
pleasure; and locked away from questioning.
They were the great: it is not greatness which

I now deny them, but the wish to prize it.
Because they squandered what they had and took,
I must grow harsh, and smear my eyes with yellow,
and hunger for the simpleness I forsook.

To Rita

I will believe the natural good survives
the childhood anguish and the grown despair;
that men and women live like me, who seek
comfort and loyalty, and the will to bear

personal unhappiness for the good they chose.
I make my testament with these the childish,
and rage a last time, but for them, against
the infection of rage and the revengeful wish.

Old friends, recall me while I dedicate
this verse to you, farewell: to them in welcome.
I who have been a master, go to school
taught by the young, because they suffer fools.
I put off bitterness to be with them,
and put their love on, and forgo your hate.

The Dejected Artist

Nothing was aimless here: the days,
some day, would mend the broken pattern
of string, and the cat's cradle
of springs, the knife in the table.

There waited a morning to give meaning
to the scrawl of colour in sprawling
hands; it needed only patience.
And we had all the happy years to wait in.

Nothing is shifted yet. No bomb
unwinds the springs, or wing
outs itself to pieces and the string.
War has overturned nothing,

but time; but waiting. To-day,
to-morrow like an ultimatum stands;
yet we cannot hurry. The welter will never
make a work now: for to-morrow stands
and is nearer, is almost here,
to pull the knife, deliberately, through the canvas.

PARIS AFTER THE WAR

Memory is the trance which can quicken, which lames.

The river bled four years; but the city was a bone.
I through that long compulsion saw them,
The sleepless in their marches, make
Engines of flesh and pulse of stone -
Animal, the machinery of shame.
I dreamt they made and saw them break them.

And now I am here again: memory compels with happiness.
The dusk takes dew, strikes fire from tenderness.
The city rings like a wing or a wire.
The wakeful at their passion shunt
On shining engines of desire;
And sleep unfolds her honey like a cunt.

THE DOUBLE PASSION

Kiss my breast or touch her ear,
Behind the passion stands a tear,
And if unshed, the conjurer is fear.

Yet if untroubled, weep no less.
The gift of terror is excess.
The gift of pity is a wilderness.

The pity is in being just.
Terror is the sleeping trust.
We with compunctions murder Will with Must,
And by compulsion make a tenderness of lust.

We speak in riddles when we love.
The tongue explores but cannot prove,
And savours meanings but at what remove.

The ambivalence of the act
Presses a mirror on the fact,
Then finds the image ominous because cracked.

No tragic gesture but its fake
Burns taller than the pain it slakes
And shakes the dark as much in dream as waking.

Kiss her breast or touch my ear:
The terror is in being near,
The pity in caressing fear,
When what employs us shames and yet is dear.

Forgive that pity rapes and chills,
Terror that it thrills and leaps.
The double passion weeps but does not kill.
Our absolution is to spill and sleep.

ANNUNCIATION

No meteor hisses and no glaciers groan
With the rush of angels beating wings on bone:
None but a correspondent telephones
That the east is turned to ice and the west to stone.

POEM AS DUET

(recorded at the Harvard Poetry Room, 1953)

What does it tell you
That a spinster of forty,
      Still handsome in flashes
      And haughty
- What does it say
      When she knits her fingers
      And blushes
And suddenly unsafe
Can no longer support
      The lingering weight of her lashes;
Because her bitten lips chafe,
And the tears are stronger than she.

A timid man past middle age
      willing to admit
      His afternoon dejection
       - Bad breath,
      Acid indigestion
      And the thought of death:
A man of middle age

Makes himself laughable
    Because he shares
    With boys of twenty
    Their despairs;
The trembling anguish of rejection,
The disappointment of plenty
And above these
    The terrible defection of love.

At first we think
The pain is in the growing older.
But no, the colder, long-delayed decay
    Is a lifetime of neglect.

A man of fifty wears a watch and chain,
A spinster walks erect,
    For neither can sustain
    The pain
    of a lifetime of neglect.

The man, the man was after all
    Not bald from birth;
The girl lacked figure
    But had some grace
    Of face –

Yet long before a paunch and denture
    Put them on the shelf
They lost the heart to launch adventure:

She could not be herself,

He could not be himself,

They had nothing but the envy,
    From the age of twelve.

No year of terror made the boy a beast,

No ignorance of life
    Unwifed the girl.

They did not lack desire,
    But fire;
Their fault was, knowing that their gifts were small.
Forgive them what they never could attempt.
    After lifetime of neglect
    Their loss of nerve

Deserves a little better than contempt:
     The state of man
     The state of woman,
The state of all mankind deserves respect.

What Did You Say?

Something in what you said strangled my wrist
And made the blood run backward. What did you say?
I heard the whisper but the sense I missed.

The sense, the desolating sense of years
And years of sense suddenly fell away.
My blood ran backward into yesterday.

Something in what you said unmanned the man
(The senses found and drowned the fallen sense)
And told the lost boy love begins again.

I was a boy again, no one had kissed
Me, happiness dazzled so that my lids were tense
As the hairspring in my boyhood wrist.

I lay among the leaves and know the place
Soft as a spring leaf where the boy had lain
In awe and passion with a crumpled face.

The falling of the leaves took thirty years
When on the instant, what did you say? It
Ran through the branches like a bliss of tears.

Something you said unmanned the fallen man
And told the boy that love begins again,
Coming with your arms flower-full of happiness,
The branches green and the leaves white with pain.

O yes, the boy remembered all that pain.

Stranger, Self and Lover

1
The stranger in my bed who slept
With strangers was at home with love,
Confident, when a woman leapt,
The hand that gave her heart a shove

Worked by way of teat and thighs.
The innocence that manned his touch
Was native as a lover's sighs
And as untutored and precise.

I could not teach the stranger much
Who had persuasion on his lips
And method at his fingertips.

2
Which of us was despicable
The stranger's blooded animal
- Or I whose introspective heart
Pumped and thumped a flood of salt

Until the act a girl desires
Was transfigured by remorse
And my kiss on teat and thighs
Tasted sweet for tasting coarse.

I could not change myself to force
The ecstasy without the pain,
The pain without the prick of shame.

3
My love, my loved, you put my hands
Together, simply and surprised.
Suddenly the self can stand
And the stranger drops his eyes.

You make the golden stranger glad
To have his brutal charm disarmed
When a girl steps into bed
Lovely, selfless and unharmed,

Teach the opposing self a lust
No more distorted by distrust,
And the inner face to smile
In welcoming its animal:

Uncaged, stranger and I are yours.
Suddenly the gauche and right,
Dissident and dexterous,
Lie in your hand, the knuckles white

And palm to palm are in your own
Intertwined to be at one.
The stranger and the self are over,
My loved, my love, you bear the lover.

OUR HANDS

Face downward in that wood and dreaming: slowly
A hand fluttered and held my nape; and as then,
I knew you in the gesture instantly
Revealed and loving. When I woke, the fine
Fingers were a leaf fallen from that same tree.

O lie, my love, in another wood and let
The leaf sink heavy, tenderly above
The smooth possessed place where my hand then met
Surrender with the passionate pressure of love.

TWO CALIFORNIAN POEMS

1
This is the coast the lemmings reached;
They did not drown but simply beached.
Here after agonies (and less)
They found the go-go star Success,
The goddess in the wilderness,
Who shook her breast and blessed the west.

She beckons from the burning-glass,
Medusa with a face of brass,
And lucid as magnesium strip
Writes with her sunset fingertip
A rain-check to the Hall of Fame:
Make a cross and put your name.

2
Blue as a dream and fabulous,
Suspended between time and space.
Here hangs, immaculate in glass,
The tropic bubble of the year that's past.

I tip the glass, and suddenly
See the snow in flurries fly:
A trick of weather in a toy
Shakes my memory with joy.
So winter used to bite, and storm
Raked me long ago and froze me warm.

ELEGIES

A man preoccupied with intellect
For forty years is thunderstruck to feel
Memory stir a different field of force.
Although I conjure Huxley and Dirac,
What works inside my head is not their terse
Delicate thrust of thought, but something odd:
The tumbling image of a man, not god,
Still unfulfilled, unhappy, yet at ease.

The women too: how strangely they survive
The fat disfigurement of time, the eyes
Hunted by haste with the feet of birds, and dark -
What I remember is the exquisite
Angelic face of trust, the head turned back
Moaning the ache of pleasure, and the hands
Flexed at the wrist shaping an agony.
How did that kernel sleep below the flesh?

What bad luck for the pair of them, the trim
White dandy and the Davenport,
To bluster with the lilac breath of youth
In brandy glasses, and defect from all
They ever valued when they knew the truth.
A little talent made them desperate -
The one to coin, the other to disgrace
The lovely gift they could not love or lose.

Always the past, the past that I despised
And now I all at once am made to eye
A visionary crocodile of tears
Parading their uninteresting fears.
All that I saw, I see now, as I saw
Was already past; and the cataract of time
That quenches the eye in milk is a cloudburst,
Crystalline, that fixes the moving past in the past.

TO HARRY, GOING WEST

Tom and Dick came out to Harry
To strike it rich, to court (and marry)
Capricious wives, and make amends
For having called their husbands friends.
Be off with you who think the best --
This is the patriotic west,

Where to receive is to be blest.
The likes of you, a solitary,
Tom and Dick came out to harry.

Each objective was agreed:
They knew the sum of human need --
The sun, the barbecue, the pool;
Strip-poker on the beach (a school
For scandal) with a one-eyed Jack;
An air-conditioned Cadillac.
Between the menace and the deed
Each objective was a greed.

Did you expect to find man kind?
All that you value has been mined.
Gold and dynamite conspire
To quench the quintessential fire,
Making a darkness so intense
It passes for indifference.
Here in the kingdom of the blind
Do you expect to find mankind?

WE THANK THEE, LORD

We thank thee, Lord, that heads of state
Are born first to be good, then great.

Thou hast preserved the innocence
Of thirty-seven presidents.

Brushed by thy burning fingertips,
Truth is a trumpet on their lips:

"Father, I cannot tell a lie"
Said one. Two hundred years went by,

And one, when earth's foundations shook,
Cried (Praise the Lord) "I'm not a crook."

Appendix: Notes on Provenance, Publication, and Revision

The poems are presented in the chronological order they were composed, where this is possible. Except where noted, the poems from Chaps. 2, 3, and 4 were intended by Bronowski to form his 'Collected Poems', as were the first two of the Christmas card poems. In Chaps. 3 and 4 several poems were intended to be included in Bronowski's other collection which did not make publication, *Thumb in the Margin*. I have followed the author's own practice in his records and marked these with (*TM*).

Chapter 2: 1928–1931 (Collected Poems)

Seascape: Notes for this poem on the subject of the nature of beauty reveal it to have been composed between 21 March and 30 April 1928. It was published in its original form in the *Cambridge Review* 16 November 1928. It was extensively revised, with changes to almost every stanza, 18 December 1933.

Betrayal: A Biography: 'Betrayal: A Biography', a poem presented in five distinct sections, was composed between 20 May and 7 September 1928, and was published in the annual review magazine *Cambridge Poetry, 1930*. The volume was published by Hogarth Press and was edited by John Davenport, Hugh Sykes Davies, and Michael Redgrave. The version printed here was 'finally revised' 23 June 1933.

Serenade: 'Serenade' was composed 1 September 1928 and published in the first edition of the magazine *Experiment*, edited by Bronowski and fellow Cambridge students including William Empson, in November 1928. The poem is ostensibly romantic but also considers the relationship between poetry and truth.

Her Lips: This poem was composed 14 September 1928 and was also published in *Experiment* in November 1928 under the title 'Poem'. The

© The Editor(s) (if applicable) and The Author(s), under exclusive license to Springer Nature Switzerland AG 2026
S. Rennie (ed.), *Jacob Bronowski: Selected Poems*,
https://doi.org/10.1007/978-3-032-19597-5

manuscript collected by Bronowski is from this volume and the only revision in the poem itself consists of changing the first letters within the quotations to upper case. The original title 'Poem' is struck through and amended to 'Her Lips'.

City Summer: The third Bronowski poem published in the first issue of *Experiment* is 'City Summer' which was written 21 September 1928. The piece was republished in *Cambridge Poetry 1929* in February of that year. The version presented here contains only very slight revisions. This poem became one of the few Bronowski pieces which was made widely available through the internet, appearing as an example of his work on the popular poetry website, *All Poetry*.

October: This poem's initial published title was 'October Casuistry'- the second word is struck out in Bronowski's collected version. It was composed between 23 September and 29 October 1928 and very heavily revised 29 December 1933. Again, Bronowski hand-writes his edits directly onto a page torn from the *Experiment* version, and every single line contains at least one revision; the final couplet is completely rewritten. It was first published in *Experiment Number 2* in February 1929, and republished in *Cambridge Poetry, 1929*, in February of that year.

To Juliet in the Tomb: Originally published as 'Juliet, dead' in *Experiment Number 3* in May 1929, this is another poem where Bronowski heavily revises his work by hand on a page from the magazine. It was composed between 19 December 1928 and 4 May 1929 and this version with the amended title was revised 24 June 1933. Interestingly, an undated transitional version with less extensive handwritten edits and the original tile retained exists in the Bronowski archives in a collected issue of the complete magazine.

Prayer: This second Bronowski poem published in *Experiment Number 3* (May 1929), was subsequently published in the 18th issue of the influential modernist literary journal *transition* in November 1929. It is a torn page from this later publication that Bronowski uses to heavily annotate his final revised version, dated 6 January 1934. The date of original composition is something of a mystery, as the author's note on this claims 29 May 1929. However, even assuming a last day of the month publication, it seems unlikely that the piece was composed and printed in less than two days to appear in *Experiment Number 3*.

Odysseus as the God of Love: This was originally published as 'Death for Odysseus' in *Experiment Number 4* in November 1929. The extensive revision is carried out on a page torn from this publication, but unusually it features, in addition to the usual handwritten annotation, examples of typewritten revisions, which have themselves subsequently been edited. This suggests at least two stages of rewriting. The original composition is dated as between 23 May and 9 November 1929 and its final revision was on 28 December 1933.

For Wilhelmina: On 25 November 1929 the publishers W. Heffer & Sons published six pamphlets containing individual poems under the series title *Songs for Sixpence*. The series was edited by Bronowski and James Reeves, the team who also co-founded *Experiment*. The subsequently eminent contributors to the *Songs for Sixpence* series were William Empson, Julian Bell, T. H. White, John Davenport, Michael Redgrave, and Bronowski himself. 'For Wilhelmina' is the title that Bronowski eventually chooses for his piece when he collects it in the 1940s, but its original title was 'For Wilhelmina, Queen of the Netherlands'. Notes for this collection state that it was originally composed between 18 March and 8 November, and finally revised 2 January 1934. Unusually, Bronowski only revises the final stanza, which he changes substantially.

Physic: 'Physic', a short, typed poem of just fifteen lines, is presented almost as an inverted Petrarchan sonnet. It is previously unpublished and was composed 5 November 1929. Bronowski's note states that it was revised 3 January 1934, but this revision appears to be just changing the first word of the eleventh line from 'But' to 'For'.

Fifth Army: This poem, containing violent imagery and offensive racial terms, was originally published in the fifth edition of *Experiment* in February 1930. As with several of Bronowski's poems, more than one phase of revision is evident, with edits made to a retained copy of the magazine, then much more extensive further revisions applied to what appears to be the original proofs. The poem was written between 20 January and 15 February and revised to this version 25 June 1933. The extent of the edits and the fact the poem was originally published so soon after composition suggest considerable investment in the piece from its author.

Return from Deaths: On at least two occasions Bronowski lists this poem between 'Fifth Army' and 'Fragments' in the 1928-31 section of his contents for his proposed *Collected Poems* volume. It is certainly written in the style from this period, composed in four discrete sections with short, varying stanza lengths and early modernist diction. However, it was only ever published in the Hull University publication, *The Torch*, in June 1936, and no exact composition date is offered. Nor is there any evidence of revision.

***Fragments: from* A Poem**: This is an unusual example of a poem that Bronowski had published, but which he chose not, or neglected, to collect. It was published in *Experiment* 6 in October 1930, where the contents page lists it as '*from* A Poem', but its page title is given as '*Fragments: from* A Poem'. There has been no revision of the original text, and there is no trace of a longer poem which this might be part of. Like Coleridge's 'Kubla Khan' and many other works, the 'fragment' claim could just be a conceit.

Tourist Season in Paris: This poem was originally published in *This Quarter* in the spring of 1932, under the title 'Speech Abroad'. *This Quarter* was a prestigious modernist magazine which ran from 1925 to 1932. This version of the poem has been heavily revised using a page from its publication, and the date given for revision is 6 January 1934. It was originally written 11 October 1930.

Ten Poems: This grouping of ten short poems of varying length and form was published in *Experiment* 7 in the spring of 1931, where its title was given simply as 'Poems'. Unusually for Bronowski for work of this period, the exact date of composition of most of the work is not provided, with 'written in the latter half of 1930' offered as an indication. However, the final poem's composition date is given as 11 January 1931. This revision, characteristically hand-written on proof pages from *Experiment*, was carried out between 28 November 1933 and 13 January 1934, with the word 'ten' added to the original title.

Her Eyes: 'Her Eyes' is an unpublished poem in four numbered sections which again features a less than precise composition date, stating simply that it was 'written Summer 1931'. The poem is very lightly revised on a typed copy but handwritten in brackets beneath the title is the note '(four poems)', which might refer to the four sections or to a putative series of poem titles beginning with 'Her…' ('Her Grief', 'Her Lips'). The revision period is given as between 4 August 1933 and 14 January 1934, but the revision on this typed out version is so light touch that there is likely to have been a handwritten original now lost.

Her Grief: This poem is not only typed onto the same paper as 'Her Eyes', but begins with those two words, supporting the suggestion that they were intended as part of a grouping. However, it remained unpublished and Bronowski's 1940s collection of his work lists just these two together in the contents page. The poem was written in August 1931 and finally (lightly) revised on the same day as the first revision of the previous poem, 4 August 1933.

Europe: This previously unpublished piece is the final poem in Bronowski's first section of his collected works, marking the point as the latest composed poem before a large selection of works which were mostly intended to be published as the volume *Thumb in the Margin*. It was written in September 1931, and it is one of the earlier of Bronowski's many works which appear to comment on contemporary geopolitical shifts. The revision consists almost entirely of excised lines, and was carried out 15th December 1933, at the end of the year Hitler became Chancellor of Germany.

CHAPTER 3: 1931–1936 (COLLECTED POEMS)

Epithalamion: This long poem, covering nine typed pages in its original version, was intended as the opening poem in the planned collection *Thumb in the Margin*. It was written between June and November 1931, and the final revision took place 30 November 1933. The revision is fairly light for much of the poem, except for on the eighth and ninth pages, where whole stanzas are excised. (*TM*)

Crisis: This political poem, composed 25 September 1931, was one of the few from this period not intended for *Thumb in the Margin*, and it was heavily revised on 4 June 1933. It is the only poem in Bronowski's files to which is attached a relatively detailed explanatory note, presumably written much later:

> This poem was written in September 1931. The National Government had recently been formed (amid the plaudits of the Sunday press, for saving the pound); and had just abandoned the Gold Standard (amid the plaudits of the

Sunday press, for saving the nation). Sir William Joynson Hicks had become Viscount Brentford. Sir Oswald Mosley had formed a Fascist party; but Hitler was still best known in England by Wyndham Lewis's partisan book. D.H. Lawrence had recently been prosecuted for obscenity. Two references in the poem are more private: one to T.S. Eliot's Oxford Anglo-Catholicism, in verse 9; and one to the poverty of research-workers, and the affluence of most undergraduates, at Cambridge and Oxford, in verse 3.

'Crisis' was published in its original form on the front page of the inaugural New Year issue of the news and literary newspaper, *Dope*, in 1932. The publication only ran for a few issues, but it was edited by the anti-fascist writer Bernard Causton (*The Moral Blitz*, Searchlight, 1941) and described itself as a 'Twentieth Century Broadsheet'. W. H. Auden would publish a poem with the same title in the *Atlantic* magazine in September 1939.

Story: This poem was published in the *Cambridge Review* 8 June 1933 and was only barely revised for this version 22 December of that year. It was written 17 November 1931. It was intended for inclusion in *Thumb in the Margin*. (*TM*)

Staring: This sonnet, containing the neologistic verb 'greeded' in the first line, is previously unpublished and was written in the spring of 1932. It was lightly revised 18 December 1933. (*TM*)

Revenge: 'Revenge', with its explanatory epigraph, was written between 4 and 20 April 1932, and finally revised, very lightly, 4 April 1933. It was published in the June 1936 edition of *The Torch*, which was the student magazine at the University of Hull, where Bronowski taught mathematics between 1934 and 1943. (*TM*)

The Sensual Law: This poem was similarly published in the June 1936 edition of *The Torch*, and it had been written in May 1933. It was revised 22 December 1933, with the whole final eleven-line stanza excised. (*TM*)

My Eyes: This third of Bronowski's poems to be published in the June 1936 edition of *The Torch* was originally composed 21 June 1933. The version in Bronowski's files is taken from the University of Hull student magazine, and though a note at the bottom states that the piece was revised on the 25 of June 1933, the original drafts are missing so there is no way of establishing the extent of revision. (*TM*)

Homer is my Example: This unpublished work consisting of five septets was originally written 5–6 December 1933, and 'finally' revised 7 December, the day after. If the typed copy in Bronowski's files is where the revision was carried out, it consists of a single excision of a single dash.

Christ: The note at the bottom of the typed copy of this poem states that it was composed 3 November 1936, nearly three years after the previous poem in Bronowski's files. This fallow creative period coincides with the first years of his post at the University of Hull, when he was not only teaching full time, but publishing scholarly geometry articles. There are only two handwritten changes to the typed copy—the original title of 'Dream' is changed to 'Christ', and the word 'Nature' has its first letter changed to lower case. (*TM*)

Criseyde: For the most part Bronowski fairly consistently orders his poetry for his putative collected works chronologically, including the *Thumb in the Margin* pieces of which this is one. However, if composition dates are to be trusted, this piece was composed a few months before the previous one, some time in March 1936. The only revision is the inclusion and excision of commas. (*TM*)

We hold our Breath: The composition date for this couplet poem is simply given as 1936, and there is no evidence of any revision. The original fair copy is simply typed onto cheap paper but there are other versions, and the inconsistently capitalised title is retained in all of them. Bronowski's habit is to capitalise non-connective words in his titles, but 'hold' here is presented all lower case. This has the effect of emphasising the capitalisation of 'Breath'. It is not clear why Bronowski groups the once again prolific period of his 1937–1940 poems separately, but this is the last of the poems in the 1931–1936 chapter, and it was not part of his intended *Thumb in the Margin* collection.

Chapter 4: 1937–1940 (Collected Poems)

Two Valentines: Originally titled separately as 'Valentine 1937' and 'Valentine 1938' this poem was apparently written in the Februarys of both of these years, with the distinction between the two dates indicated by a comma in the note at the bottom of the typed draft. Although both sections are seven lines long the first part consists of two short stanzas and the second of three stanzas is presented on a different page, perhaps representing each of the 'two Valentines'. I have indicated this gap with an ellipsis break in this publication.

The Gangster: This previously unpublished political poem consisting of seven quatrains was written 6 July 1937, and the typed version held in Bronowski's files contains only minimal handwritten revision. It is composed in dense quatrains on the theme of political strongmen and their public allure, with particular reference to cinematic tropes. (*TM*)

The Sleeping and the Dead: Consisting of three octets, with varying lineation and frequent enjambment, 'The Sleeping and the Dead' was written 20 September 1937, although the month 'August' is crossed out in the note. Certainly, the poem appears as a fair copy with no evident revisions. (*TM*)

Take Your Gun: 'Take Your Gun' is another political poem with no evident revision presented as fair copy typed on cheap paper. It was written 22 October 1937 and subsequently published in *New Writing* magazine in the autumn of 1938. *New Writing* was edited by a former Cambridge contemporary of the author's, John Lehmann, and this poem became one of the few Bronowski pieces which was made widely available through the internet, appearing, along with 'City Summer', as an example of his work on the popular poetry website, *All Poetry*. However, it was not one of the poems included in *Poems for Spain* (1939), as claimed by Bronowski's biographer, Timothy Sandefur, in *The Ascent of Jacob Bronowski* (2019). (*TM*)

Guadalajara: This is the first of four Spanish Civil War poems printed and published as a pamphlet by the Andrew Marvell Press in Hull in 1939 (the others are 'The Death of Garcia Lorca', 'Greece and Spain', and 'Bomber'). The pamphlet was titled *Spain 1939: Four Poems* and was produced with a plain cover. 'Guadalajara' was one of Bronowski's most widely published poems, at least during his own lifetime, also appearing in the aforementioned Autumn 1938 edition of *New Writing*, and the volume *Poems for Spain* (Hogarth Press) in 1939. The latter publication was again edited by John Lehmann along with Stephen Spender. 'Guadalajara' was written on New Year's Eve 1937. (*TM*)

The Death of Garcia Lorca: Also included in the Hogarth Press's *Poems for Spain* in 1939 was this poem on the topic of the 1936 assassination of the Spanish poet and playwright Frederico Garcia Lorca (1998–1936) by Nationalist militia. It was written 22 December 1937, but no evidence of revision is apparent from Bronowski's records.

Greece and Spain: Consisting of nine quatrains, this poem was the last to be composed but the third in the sequence of pieces included in *Spain 1939: Four Poems*. Again, there is no evidence of revision, and this is the only one of the works from the Spanish volume that Bronowski did not include in his intended wider collection *Thumb in the Margin*. It was written in the August of 1838.

Bomber: The final piece in *Spain 1939: Four Poems* was written in July 1938. It is formally unusual for this composition period in that it is composed in rhyming couplets, although several of these are half rhymes in the manner of W. H. Auden. It does not appear to have been published elsewhere. (*TM*)

Birthday Ode: This poem's title has been amended on the extant typescript from 'for Eirlys's Birthday 3. January 1938.' to simply 'Birthday Ode'. The brief note at the bottom of the page states 'January 1938'. Eirlys Roberts was Bronowski's long-term girlfriend at the time the poem was originally composed but he had already met his future wife, the artist Rita Coblentz. Despite the romantic history of the poem, Bronowski intended the piece for his *Thumb in the Margin* collection, with no revision other than its title. (*TM*)

You Sought the Shadow: Presented as five septets with a consistent rhyme scheme of ABABCCB 'You Sought the Shadow' is only lightly revised in the extant typescript copy, with a few adjustments to punctuation and changes of tense. A brief note at the bottom of the page indicates that it was composed in June 1938. (*TM*)

God: Reflecting the continuing development of Bronowski's humanist philosophy, this Petrarchan sonnet is sardonically addressed to the divine. It contains revision only in its concluding sestet, where the eleventh line has been almost completely rewritten. Formally, its most notable element is that whilst the opening octet adheres strictly to the centuries-old Petrarchan rhyme scheme ABBAABBA, the sestet uses no discernible rhyme at all, perhaps reflecting the breakdown of political order that the poem arguably alludes to. The poem was written in November 1938. (*TM*)

Victory: This deeply ironic work on the subject of the Battle of Ebro during the Spanish Civil War was written 3 January 1939, just two months after the victory of General Franco's forces. The battle was the largest of the war, and it was disastrous for the Republican campaign which Bronowski and many British intellectuals supported. The typed copy contains just one revision, changing the twenty-fourth line from 'And when the general flies' to the more vernacular 'And when the general lords it'.

Not All Lose Hope: Composed shortly after 'Victory' on 23 January 1939, this more optimistic poem on the subject of the Spanish Civil War is presented as five tercets and one quatrain, with the former following an ABA rhyme scheme, similar to the *terza rima* form. The piece is moderately revised on the evidence of this typed version. (*TM*)

The Death of Karl Kraus: Karl Kraus, the Austrian journalist, poet, and satirist died of natural causes in 1936, so this is less an elegy than a reflection on the subsequent *Anschluss,* the annexation of Austria by Nazi forces in 1938, and the threat of Europe-wide fascism. The poem, barely revised in the version in Bronowski's records, was composed 25 January 1939. (*TM*)

The Death of Pius XI: Written in loosely single-rhymed tercets, this poem was begun just four days after the death of the Pope Pius XI (1957-1939), with a note stating that it was written between 14 and 24 February. The poem is critical of the pragmatic 'concordats' that Pius signed with the likes of Hitler and Mussolini, with the word 'peace', featured in the first and last lines, appearing synonymous with appeasement. Much of the poem is moderately revised but the whole of the seventh stanza has been rewritten. (*TM*)

The Bullfight: This poem was written between 16 and 24 February 1939 and has been selectively revised, with some long stanzas left untouched, while the fourth has had three lines excised from it. In this prolific composition period this work eschews the rhymes of the previous few to be presented in unrhymed stanzas. (*TM*)

In Memory of Ramon Lull: Bronowski Anglicises the surname, but this poem celebrates the thirteenth-century philosopher and poet Ramon Llull (1232-1316). Llull was associated with the island of Majorca, where Bronowski had previously spent considerable time with Robert Graves and Laura Riding. The poem was composed 6 March 1936, and its closing stanzas refer slyly to Llull's 'Italian pupil Bruno'. 'Bruno' or course, was the name by which Bronowski was always known. (*TM*)

The Death of W. B. Yeats: This poem is a rather more conventional elegy, in that it was written 11 March 1939, just over month after Yeats's death. The poem is composed in ten couplet quatrains, although originally there were twelve and the fourth and fifth are struck through in the typescript. The poem is celebratory of Yeats's legacy, and it makes cultural connections between its subject's Irishness and the writer's Jewishness. (*TM*)

The Heroic Moment: 'The Heroic Moment', a late poem on the subject of the Spanish conflict, was composed between the 27 and 28 March 1939. Formally, it consists of ten quatrains and two sestets, fifty-two lines in all. It has a consistent alternating rhyme scheme throughout, although many are loose half-rhymes. Only the last three stanzas are revised, with the tenth quatrain being almost completely rewritten. The title is handwritten on the typescript and appears to be added subsequently.

The Great: Another poem with the title handwritten after the fact, 'The Great' is also a work which contains allusions to other poets, including Yeats, Dryden, Goethe, Milton, and Cervantes. The poem's subject appears to be the geopolitical moment and a reflection on the political engagement of a range of European writers—even the English pamphleteer William Cobbett (1763–1835) gets a mention. It was written 22 April 1939 and in the edited typescript in Bronowski's files, the third of its original nine quatrains is entirely struck through. Other revisions are minor, but the third (once fourth) stanza's final line is crossed out and a new first line is inserted, changing the line order. (*TM*)

Some Happy Hours: 'Some Happy Hours' is again titled in handwriting on a previously typed page, and the poem contains very minimal revision consisting of changes of articles or single words. It was written during the very productive period on 17 June 1939, and represents a return to a more personal, introspective poetic approach. (*TM*)

The Death of Ernst Toller: This poem was originally titled 'Elegy for Ernst Toller', but the handwritten changing of the heading to 'The Death of Ernst Toller' better reflects the poem's focus as less a celebration of the German Marxist playwright's life, than a contemplation of the circumstances surrounding his suicide on May 22 in a New York hotel. Toller had been a passionate supporter of the Spanish Republican cause, and in another example of Bronowski's poetic topics being mirrored by W. H. Auden, that poet published an elegy for Toller in 1940. Bronowski's poem was written 2 July 1939, and the typescript indicates only light revision. (*TM*)

To the Fallen: While so much of Bronowski's previous poetry had been on the subjects of the violent conflicts of the preceding years, this poem, written 11 July 1939, is addressed to the future victims of the global conflict which only the most optimistic observers believed might not happen. It is moderately revised, and it consists of six quatrains composed in alternating half rhymes. (*TM*)

The Impersonal Tragedy: Composed 25 July 1939, with very little subsequent revision, this is another poem on the subject of the impending global conflict, but this time the piece offers a despairing Freudian *casus belli*, declaring that 'Oedipus [swings] in the circle of his pain'. Again, the focus of the poem is on the individuals who will suffer the consequences of destruction. Interestingly, the alternating rhymes which characterise this period of Bronowski's composition are much truer in this piece, perhaps reflecting the deterministic interpretation of political events. (*TM*)

Alexander's Drum: Written just three days after 'The Impersonal Tragedy', 28 July 1939, this poem is again on the subject of the looming conflict, but it blends classical, historical, and literary references into its content. Morris's utopian novel *News from Nowhere* is wryly presented as a source as worthy as the

British parliamentary record, *Hansard*, and the final reference is to the famously incongruous eighteenth-century conflict, The War of Jenkins' Ear. It was initially composed in ten quatrains with only the final two lines of each stanza rhyming, but along with other revisions, the original seventh stanza is entirely struck through. (*TM*)

The Word: Marking yet another poetic approach to the future European war, 'The Word' was written the day after 'Alexander's Drum', 29 July 1939, making that month probably the most productive in Bronowski's poetic career. The poem considers the power of speech in igniting political conflagrations and is composed in closely rhyming couplet stanzas. Originally there were thirteen couplets, but the eleventh is struck through. (*TM*)

Our Age is Beginning: Composed 14 August 1939, this barely revised poem is again written with closely rhymed couplets but this time it consists of relatively long stanzas, and the meter is fairly consistently iambic tetrameter. The topic moves away from war to a contemplation of future technological achievement, interestingly, diverging from the 'Great Man' approach to history and praising the manual skill of the mechanic, the craftsman, and the 'navvy'. Although perhaps inspired by Britain's drive towards self-sufficiency in the run-up to war (market gardens and allotments are referred to), there is an optimism in this poem which offers early glimpses of the humanistic thesis of Bronowski's future *Ascent of Man* project. (*TM*)

War and Peace: This sardonically aphoristic poem is composed in rhyming couplet stanzas, and is one of the shortest from this period, at just fourteen lines once the struck through original sixth stanza is removed. It was written 30 August 1939 and, though it makes reference to war, it is more a condemnation of profiteering, recognising that the rich have the means to benefit whatever the global situation. (*TM*)

The Bigot: Consisting of seventeen five-line stanzas, 'The Bigot' is technically the first Bronowski poem of the new decade, having been written between 13 November 1939 and 1 January 1940. Along with allusion to familiar figures including Blake, Kraus and the pope, the nineteenth-century writers Wordsworth and Browning are referred to. The poem again addresses economic injustice, but there is a more personal contemplation of the speaker's relationship with social issues and activism.

A Day at the Races: This twelve-line poem, presented in quatrains with only the second and fourth line of every stanza rhyming, is deliberately light in register with a bouncing iambic meter. It appears to compare the financial market to the betting industry. There is an oblique reference to Jonathon Swift's Houyhnhnm characters in *Gulliver's Travels* (1726), but in this case the horses are not Swift's rational beings, but ignorant of the reason they race.

Prologue and Epilogue: Both sections of this poem are headed with a statement that they are 'for a Living Newspaper on 'Oil'". The Living Newspaper form, where current events are recited to a live theatrical audience, is a now-obscure modernist phenomenon popularised in the late 1930s, but Bronowski's conceit frames his poem as a commentary on the contemporary oil business.

The piece is presented as two discrete parts consisting of four quatrains, and it begins with a reference to T. E. Lawrence's (1888–1935) efforts on behalf of the British government to secure relations with Arabian powers. It was composed 1 April 1940.

The Thumb in the Margin: The eponymous final poem of Bronowski's mooted collection originally consisted of thirty-one sestets, making it easily the most substantial work of this period, even with three of those stanzas struck through during the very extensive revision the piece underwent. It is also Bronowski's most self-critical and personally revealing poem, sharing some similarities with the confessional poetry which would eventually be fashionable in the 1950s and 1960s. It was composed through February and March of 1940. (*TM*)

CHAPTER 5: 1939–1973 CHRISTMAS CARD POEMS

These poems, which Bronowski referred to variously as 'Christmas poems' or occasionally 'seasonal poems', were part of a joint venture for Bronowski and his wife Rita Coblentz Bronowski, to distribute annually to friends and family. The tradition lasted for almost a quarter of a century, and the arrival of the cards, with original poems by Bronowski and original illustrations by Rita, were eagerly anticipated by recipients. Some of the poems were published without the artwork separately in magazines and other publications, but only after they had appeared in the cards. *Ambit* published ten of them as 'Ten Christmas Poems' in 1963/64 and two in 1966. *The San Diego Magazine* published eight together in 1969. Bronowski also included two in his book *Science and Human Values* in 1965, and one each his radio programmes *The Imaginative Mind in Science* (1964) and the *Abacus and the Rose* (1965).

The poems vary in their themes but are mostly sonnet-like in scale and composed in a bouncing iambic tetrameter. They began in 1939 and continued until the year before Bronowski's death, 1973. None were produced during the war years 1941–1946, nor 1950 and 1959, for personal reasons. Two years saw two cards produced—1939 and 1947. In 2013, Bronowski's daughter, Judith Bronowski, brought the 'Bronowski Christmas Cards' together in a self-published illustrated book for the family. The great advantage of this was that it allowed the works to be viewed in their original graphic and textual state, with Rita's illustrations reproduced across the page from their associated text. In her preface, Judith explains the process of production:

Each year Bruno (Jacob) wrote his annual poem reflecting on a topic of personal or political significance. This poem was printed on small (4.5 × 6.25 inches) white folded cardstock. Rita then created the cover illustration. She cut a linoleum block and then hand-printed and painted her interpretation of the poem's theme.

Eventually hundreds of cards were being mailed across the world and a portion of the family home was turned into a printing workshop each winter.

Apparently, Rita would always wait for her husband to compose the poem before she designed and produced the illustration based on the verse's theme. The Bronowski holdings at Jesus College, Cambridge contain many versions and revisions of the Christmas poems, and some years the final poem was not completed until perilously close to the postal deadline. Those for 1957 and 1958 were actually composed in the first week of December. Judith worked with Bronowski's own versions of the cards which, characteristically, contained some small revisions handwritten directly onto the cards themselves. These are reproduced in her book, and I have used these 'final' copies, in keeping with the rest of the poems in this collection, as the basis for the versions offered here. The last poem to be revised is the one from 1972, indicating that Bronowski was still intent on improving his literary works at this point. Indeed, a note in the author's hand on a typed list of the Christmas poems ending with the 1969 entry which reads 'Query: have all these been included in "Collected Poems" yet' suggests that Bronowski never lost hope of a complete poetic works being published at some point. Apart from the 1939 poems, Bronowski also noted an exact composition date for each of the poems, clearly taken from the exhaustive appointments diary he had kept for many years, which assiduously detailed his creative practice. I have provided these dates, and publication details, for each poem below, with first lines included for ease of reference.

1939: Now good King Carol turns his ass—November 1939 (*TM*)

1939b: It was no star the Magi heard—November 1939 (*TM*)

1940: Jupiter and Saturn played—29 November 1940—(*Science and Human Values*, 1956)

1947: The voice of God that spoke and struck—12 September 1947—(*Ambit* 18 1963/64; *Science and Human Values*, 1956)

1947b: Between the olive and the sloe—29 September 1947

1948: Beyond the manger shines the tree—29 October 1948—(*San Diego Magazine* Vol. 22, 2 December 1969)

1949: Everything was snow and gold—6 November 1949

1951: No apparition drowned the air—23 November 1951—(*Ambit* 18 1963/64)

1952: The snoring man, the peevish moke—8 November 1952

1953: Under the raging equinox—30 November 1953—(*Ambit* 18 1963/64)

1954: A landscape where the scrub disdains—13 July 1954—(*Ambit* 18 1963/64; *San Diego Magazine* Vol. 22, 2 December 1969)

1955: An ice age and a rage of heat—19 November 1955

1956: The desert is a rose, and glows—26 November 1956—(*Ambit* 18 1963/64)

1957: Snow should have fallen upward to eclipse—3 December 1957—(*Ambit* 18 1963/64)

1958: Faster than light and cold as absolute—5 December 1958—(*Ambit* 18 1963/64; *The Imaginative Mind in Science*, 1964 [radio programme])

1960: I, having built a house, reject—11 November 1960—(*Ambit* 18 1963/64; *The Abacus and the Rose*, 1965 [radio play])

1961: It was a star, it was a bird—28 November 1961

1962: There must have been a time when fate—29 August 1962—(*Ambit* 18 1963/64; *San Diego Magazine* Vol. 22, 2 December 1969)

1963: Aquinas argued how an arrow flies—28 September 1963—(*Ambit* 18 1963/64)

1964: Blue as a dream and fabulous—15 November 1964—(*Ambit* 22 1966; *San Diego Magazine* Vol. 22, 2 December 1969)

1965: This is the coast the lemmings reached—23 November 1965—(*Ambit* 22 1966; *San Diego Magazine* Vol. 22, 2 December 1969)

1966: One of the magi brought, to match—30 November 1966—(*San Diego Magazine* Vol. 22, 2 December 1969)

1967: He wore sandals and a beard—14 November 1967—(*San Diego Magazine* Vol. 22, 2 December 1969)

1968: Beyond the walls of dogma bloom—30 October 1968—(*San Diego Magazine* Vol. 22, 2 December 1969)

1969: Clap your hands and reach your toes—28 November 1969

1970: Again the desert redeploys—2 November 1970

1971: Always in flight, pell mell, farewell—19 November 1971

1972: Genetics has a monkish rule—12 September 1972

1973: With what contempt the Scots defined—25 October 1973

Chapter 6: 1939–1974 Other Poems

[**The images of violence**]: Although it was written in March 1939, during one of Bronowski's most prolific composition periods, this untitled poem was not included in its author's intended retrospective of his work in the early 1940s, and so it begins this later chapter. There is a single revision on the typescript consisting of the word 'has' in the fifth line replaced with the word 'takes'. The typescript is signed at the base in Bronowski's hand. The poem builds from open verse to rhyming couplets, and its subject, like so many pieces from this period, is war and political violence.

[**Her body**]: Also not intended for the wider collection its author was planning, ['Her body…'] was written 24 March 1939, and might be classed as part of the series of poems beginning or titled with that female pronoun. Again, the typescript features a handwritten signature and there are no revisions evident.

[**Now the turbulent lives**]: This is another signed but untitled poem from the spring of that year, dated 29 May 1939. It is presented in loosely rhymed quatrains, and with its references to rifle-sights and the explosive thermite alongside its musings about the state of humanity, it offers a pessimistic view of the immediate future.

[**Slowly the abscess**]: This untitled piece was written 26 July 1939 in the same form as ['Now the turbulent lives…'], with quatrains loosely rhyming just the second and fourth lines. Although six quatrains appear on the typescript the final one ends without punctuation. Rather than the author's usual striking through, there is an editing line which indicates that this final stanza should be excised. The reason for this becomes apparent when the following poem, ['To Rita'], begins with this final stanza. The current piece is edited down to just five stanzas. Bronowski makes the common error of spelling 'abscess' in this poem without the first 's'. I have taken the decision to correct this error in the belief that Bronowski would have done so with further editing.

To Rita: Beginning with the excised final quatrain of the previous poem, and written on the same day of 26 July 1939, this Petrarchan sonnet is titled 'To Rita' in handwritten black ink, unlike the blue ink that provides the composition date at the bottom of the typescript.

The Dejected Artist: This poem is the last of the group of 1939 compositions which were not included in their author's intended collection, and apparently the last piece written before an extended creative hiatus through WWII. It is dated 30 December 1939 and at the bottom of the piece, unusually, the typed 'J. Bronowski.' is followed by 'for Rita Colin.'

Paris after the War: Composed 31 October 1946, this poem begins with a single line which may be read as an epigraph, but it then proceeds to two sestets with shifting rhyme structures. It is signed 'JB' and exists only as a handwritten copy, unedited. Although it is used in its literal sense within a simile, the closing expletive is atypical of Bronowski's style, perhaps registering the shock of the new post-war age.

The Double Passion: This poem, again signed with initials, was written 9 September 1947. It contains no revision but when transcribing the piece, I initially followed what I thought were capitalisations of abstract nouns including 'Passion', 'Pity' and 'Pain'. This device was common in poetry of the time (W. H. Auden used it extensively), but unusual for Bronowski. I eventually realised that the typewriter used for this typescript was faulty, and that it effectively capitalised all letter 'Ps'. The possibility remained that these were intended capitalisations, but the uncapitalised abstract noun 'terror', used in the same formation as 'pity' in the following line in the first quatrain, suggested otherwise.

Annunciation: This monorhymed quatrain, dated 28 November 1947, is unusual in that the typescript has been folded and torn into half a page from its original foolscap iteration. The poem is in the aphoristic style of some of the Christmas poems, and it wryly registers the increasing geopolitical tensions of the beginnings of the Cold War.

Poem as Duet: Although this poem's typescript does not include the date of the composition, a note in parenthesis below the title indicates that it was 'recorded at the Harvard Poetry Room, 1953'. This presumably refers to a performance in the famed George Edward Woodbury Poetry Room in Harvard University Library—Bronowski was teaching at the Massachusetts Institute of Technology in Cambridge, Mass. that year, funded by the Carnegie Foundation. It is an atypical Bronowski piece in both theme and form. Its subject at first appears to be a third-person narrative of a difficult middle-aged romance, but this becomes a statement on gender and wider humanity at the close. The extensive use of pronounced indentation is also unusual for Bronowski.

What Did You Say?: This poem was composed 18 July 1955 and formally it is a play on the villanelle form, but with twenty-three rather than nineteen lines and variations on the rhyme scheme in the six tercet stanzas. By this time the villanelle was in the spotlight because of Dylan Thomas's 'Do not go gentle into that good night' composed in that form. The Bronowski's had been reacquainted with Thomas in Massachusetts in 1953, shortly before the Welsh poet died.

Stranger, Self, and Lover: Composed between 23 July and 23 August 1955, 'Stranger, Self and Lover' appears in more than one typescript form in Bronowski's files, but none of them give any indication of revision. The poem is in three sections with quatrain and tercet stanzas, and the rhymes alternate between half and full, with shifting schemes.

Our Hands: 'Our Hands' consists of just nine lines in two stanzas, and it was composed 25 August 1955. It is one of several Bronowski poems whose title begins with a possessive pronoun, and like many of them it has a romantic theme. It might also be noted that it has a *Romantic* theme as well, with the speaker lying daydreaming in a wood, like that of John Keats's 'Ode to a Nightingale' (1819).

Two Californian Poems: These two poems, repurposed from Christmas card verses, were published on the same page in the British poetry magazine *Ambit* (1959–2023) 28 November 1966. Bronowski's files contain a page taken from the magazine but there is also an earlier handwritten version of the first of these poems dated 23 November 1965. The only differences between this and the printed version is that the ampersands are written as full 'ands'.

Elegies: 'Elegies', which is a single poem apparently on the subject of elegies, rather than being one itself, is unusually handwritten on graph paper, indicating that this is a first draft, along with the note at the top which reads 'begun 4 November 1968 in Detroit'. However, the poem is written in a confident hand which suggests that it might be close to a fair copy, and there are no revisions.

To Harry, Going West: The note at the bottom of this poem states that it was written 'June 1967 and November 1969', indicating that the final date was a period of revision. The poem consists of a nine-line stanza followed by two octets, and apart from the extra rhyme in the first stanza, it is composed in quite straightforward rhyming couplets. This gives it a light, playful register, and indeed the subject of the poem appears to contain elements of social satire. Bronowski retained a rejection letter relating to the submission of this poem to the *Atlantic* magazine. In it, the then editor of the publication, Robert Manning (1919–2012) calls the poem 'clever and more than that', but suggests 'it doesn't just work out for the magazine'.

We Thank Thee, Lord: The date on the handwritten draft of this satirical poem, 4 March 1974, three months before Bronowski's death, perhaps indicates that it was the last poem he wrote. It is certainly a piece that is occasional, as it is clearly a commentary on the Watergate scandal of that period, ending with President Nixon's famous declaration 'I'm not a crook'. Even though the poem consists of just five rhyming couplet stanzas, the draft contains revisions to almost every line. There are three separate typewritten versions which further contain the same brief revisions. This would indicate that Bronowski had expectations that this piece would be published at some point in the future.

INDEX[1]

---

[1] Note: Page numbers followed by 'n' refer to notes.